FELIXSTOWE
A Pictorial History

The old battery and the temporary church of St John the Baptist in August 1888. In the foreground beside the Eastward Ho estate office is the site of the Town Hall built four years later, and in the background are the first buildings in Sea Road.

FELIXSTOWE
A Pictorial History

Robert Malster

Phillimore

1992

Published by
PHILLIMORE & CO. LTD.
Shopwyke Hall, Chichester, Sussex

ISBN 0 85033 830 1

Printed and bound in Great Britain by
BIDDLES LTD.
Guildford, Surrey

List of Illustrations

Frontispiece: The old battery and Sea Road, 1888

Preface and Acknowledgements

My earliest memories of Felixstowe are of visits to an aunt living there in those halcyon days before the Second World War. We arrived by train at Beach station and set out to walk to where she lived at the southern end of the town, that part which George Tomline had hoped would become the new Felixstowe of the late 19th century.

I knew nothing of the redoubtable Colonel Tomline then; I recall only the parrot that sat on a perch outside a shop on our route from the station. It is only in more recent times that my delvings into local history have introduced me to such characters as George Tomline and John Chevallier Cobbold and to the story of their influence on the town that grew up to become one of the most popular resorts on the east coast, particularly after the Empress of Germany chose it for a family holiday in 1891.

Although it can be claimed that this book is the first attempt to set down the history of the town in this form, I am very much aware that I follow many others who have researched the town's past. There is S. D. Wall, who contributed so much of his researches to the *Felixstowe Times*, and there is Alan Jobson, who did the same. Cynthia Park produced *The Cotman Walk* for the Felixstowe Society, an organisation that has done a great deal in recent years to promote the care of the town's older buildings, and Phil Hadwen, Ray Twidale and Peter White, joined later by Graham Henderson, John Smith and Neil Wylie, have followed in the footsteps of Charles Corker by publishing fine books of photographs of the town both from their postcard collections and from the extraordinary store of negatives left by Charles Emeny and his sons, William and Clement.

Nobody who looks seriously at the history of the area can fail to be impressed by the records of the Emeny family, who for almost a century documented the history of Felixstowe and its people. Charles Emeny was taking photographs as early as 1867, when he was a young man of 18, and before very long he had gone into the photographic trade with a shop in Walton High Street. His son, Clement, retired only in 1950, and the business was carried on until 1967 by Mr. B. C. Mason. It goes without saying that many of the pictures in this book were taken by the Emenys.

Many peope have assisted me with the writing of this book and with assembling the illustrations. My thanks go to Mrs. Gladys Wilton, Mrs. Valerie Norrington, the late Charles Corker, the late Harry Wilton, David Cleveland, Geoff Cordy, Robert Diamond, Charles Hall, Dave Kindred, Gordon Kinsey, Peter Northeast, Norman Scarfe, the editor of the *East Anglian Daily Times*, Ken Rice, the staff of the Suffolk Record Office, and many more who have helped me either with the loan of photographs, with information and advice, or in other ways. Without them this book could never have been produced.

   Photographs have very generously been provided by the following, whom I thank for their help: Mrs. Gladys Wilton and John Wilton, 9-11, 15, 16, 24, 34, 35, 40, 41, 44-46, 50-52, 56-61, 63, 65, 67, 69-73, 75, 77, 79-81, 86, 88-95, 97, 98, 110, 134, 135, 137, 138; Mrs. Valerie Norrington, 2, 3; David Cleveland, 62; *East Anglian Daily Times*, 33, 68, 111, 124, 133, 167-70; East Anglian Film Archive, 146; Felixstowe Dock and Railway Company, 28, 29, 164-66; Charles Hall, 157-59; Oscar and Peter Johnson, the Lowndes Gallery, London, 108; Peter Kent, 126, 127; Dave Kindred, 4-8, 12, 13, 17-20, 25-27, 30, 36-38, 47, 49, 53, 66, 82-85, 101-4, 109, 116, 117, 119, 120; Gordon Kinsey, 42, 76, 115, 118, 121, 122, 125, 136, 139-45, 147-49, 151, 153-56, 160, 161; Mrs. Marion Leeson, 78; Miss Pat O'Driscoll, 162, 163; Suffolk Record Office, 39, 87, 99, 105, 106, 112-14. All other photographs are from the author's collection.

Introduction

Although the name of Felixstowe is often said to be derived from St Felix, the Burgundian monk who brought Christianity to the Anglo-Saxon kingdom of East Anglia in the seventh century, the town that we know as Felixstowe does not have a very long history, having grown up in the 19th and early 20th centuries largely as a result of the fashion for sea bathing and seaside holidays.

The Romans were here in the third century A.D., when they built one of their Saxon Shore forts at Walton, about a mile south of the mouth of the River Deben. A Roman road seems to have linked the fort with Pye Street, the main road from Colchester to Venta Icenorum, near Norwich, and it is possible that the name Stratton Hall (Straet-tun) in Trimley refers to this road.

After the Norman Conquest, Hugh Bigod, a member of the family that established its headquarters at Framlingham, built his castle in the corner of the Roman walls, which he used as the outer defences of the new fortification. But in the 1170s Henry II had Walton Castle dismantled following Bigod's participation in the barons' rebellion of 1173-74. According to John Kirby's *Suffolk Traveller*, 'this was so effectually done that, to prevent its ever rising again, the stones of it were carried into all parts of Felixstow, Walton and Trimly; and footpaths were paved with them, on both sides of the road'.

Parts of the foundations of the Saxon Shore fort were still to be seen, 187 yards in length, in about 1740, but coastal erosion was even then finishing the work of Henry's 12th-century engineers. The sea has since completed the destruction of the remains, though Roman masonry can still be seen just off 'the Dip' at very low tides.

It is said to have been within the walls of the fort that Felix set up the headquarters of his East Anglian bishopric. Here, and not at Dunwich, say some authorities, was Domnoc. Throughout the Anglo-Saxon period, however, the name Burgh was used for the Walton fortress, and in Domesday Book Old Felixstowe is called Burch. Part of this settlement was known in the 14th century as Fylthestowe, a name which signifies a holy place, or a meeting place, where hay grows, and it was from this that the town's name grew. There was indeed a meeting place for the Hundred of Colneis at the south end of Walton, and Walton had an ancient church dedicated to St Felix that was given in the 11th century to Rochester Priory, which established a subordinate priory of St Felix at Walton.

The land on which the town of Felixstowe was to rise formed part of the Manor of Walton, one of a number in Suffolk held by the Bigod family, and of a smaller manor with which Roger Bigod endowed the priory. The Manor of Felixstowe Priory remained separate long after the Dissolution. The administrative centre of the Manor of Walton and the residence of the Bigods when in the area seems to have been what is now known as the Old Hall, of which the ruins were partly excavated in the 1960s.

Norman Scarfe points out that whether the name Walton is interpreted as the tun or farmstead of the Welshmen, the Romano-British, or as the tun 'near the wall', the Roman fort, it is likely to indicate an early settlement, one of the earliest in Suffolk.

Walton is indeed the predominant settlement in the early history of this corner of Suffolk. The manor at Walton was, to judge from an account of the revenues in 1228, a very profitable one comprising 50 very small but thriving estates farmed by the successors of the small groups of freemen appearing in the Domesday survey. Scattered throughout the Colneis Hundred, the names of these estates survive today in farmhouses and farms such as Morston Hall, Grimston Hall, Kembroke Hall, Candlet, Gulpher and Alston Hall.

From Grimston Hall in Trimley St Martin came Thomas Cavendish, who in 1586 sailed on a two-year expedition that took his little fleet of three small ships around the world. Cavendish, whose forebears appear in local records as Candish or Caundishe, set out on a second privateering expedition in 1591 but failed to get through the Straits of Magellan; he died on the voyage home.

Walton's Quaker Community

In the mid-17th century Walton seems to have been strongly affected by the preaching of George Whitehead, one of 'the Valiant Sixty' then spreading Quakerism across the country. He first came to Suffolk in 1655, but it was not until 1659, after a short spell in Ipswich gaol, that he held meetings at Walton and Trimley. There were soon active Quakers in the vicinity.

The young daughter of one of them, Sarah Fryer, died on 14 January 1660,

> and on the 16 day of the same month we having no burring place of our own we carried the Body to Harwich to be buried But the Mayor Milles Hubbard and the townesmen, in their Rage and madness took the body from us and sent it backe againe and sett it on the sea shoore upon the stones and so left wher it remained for some time unburied.

When another Quaker, Thomas Pinson, died at Walton on 28 January that year, 'we carried that body to Harwich againe wher quietly wee burriee the Corps'. Thomas Pinson, or another of the same name, had the previous year been fined the considerable sum of £57 for failing to pay tithe of £14 1s.

Faced with such enmity, and in view of their belief, contrary to the established Church, that it was not necessary to bury their dead in consecrated ground, it is no surprise to find Joseph and James Lilley being 'buried in ther garden at Falkenham' and Jo Stebbing of Trimley 'buried in his own hempland' rather than being carried to Harwich. In December 1662, however, Matthew Seaman's child, Ann, was 'burried in Jos. Scotts burring place being the first body'. When Joseph Scott junior died in 1675 the Friends acquired the property, and between then and 1750 more than 100 Quakers were interred in the little plot beside what had become their meeting house.

1. Walton Ferry, where travellers from Harwich came ashore to visit the defences at Landguard Fort, is seen in this watercolour painted by Thomas Rowlandson in 1808. A ferry has continued to run from Felixstowe to Harwich in recent years, though its future is in doubt.

2. Pond Cottages in Seaton Road, demolished in 1949. The Quaker Meeting House was on the right, behind the cyclist.

3. The site of the Quaker Meeting House and burial ground as it is now. The electricity pole on the left and the ventilator pipe on the right can also be identified in the earlier photograph of Pond Cottages.

4. A view of Walton Street taken in November 1877. The road surface was obviously extremely soft.

5. Buildings in High Street, Walton, photographed in February 1878. The building with the shop windows is now a flower shop; at one time it belonged to the International Tea Company.

6. Also taken in February 1878, this photograph is titled 'Back of Horns Farm', which was in Brook Lane. At that time Mrs. Sarah Horne was listed as a farmer at Felixstowe.

7.   Joseph Horne had been at the *Angel Inn* in Walton High Street in the 1850s, but at the time this photograph was taken towards the end of the century the licensee was Frederick Brinkley, probably a member of the family that produced the celebrated ferrymen at Felixstowe Ferry. The *Angel* closed in 1937.

8.   This photograph of Walton High Street was taken in 1888, the year after a Local Board had been formed to administer both Walton and Felixstowe.

9. Felixstowe Lodge, built by the eccentric Philip Thicknesse out of a fisherman's cottage. In this print of *c*.1830 one of the martello towers built in 1808-10 can be seen to the left.

10. A photograph of Felixstowe Lodge taken in 1854, when it was a seaside home of John Chevallier Cobbold.

Seaside Resort

Eighteenth-century medical men discovered the advantages of sea bathing, and the first bathing machines were in use at such places as Deal and Lowestoft well before the end of the century, but Felixstowe was not immediately affected by the fashion for spending the summer by the sea. At the extremity of the Colneis peninsula, it was cut off from Ipswich and the rest of Suffolk by a road that was, at best, a rough one.

When David Elisha Davy came this way in search of church inscriptions in 1829 he found:

> rather a busy scene; considerable preparations making for receiving company; many temporary stables just above the beach, for occasional parties who come in considerable numbers from the country around to dine & spend the day: when I was here about 3 years ago, I recollect but two of these booths, & I now found a large addition to them. In addition to these, there are two, if not more, very good houses, where parties may obtain accommodation for the day, or for a longer time, at a very reasonable expence ... The place seems to be in a very thriving condition, many new houses have been built, & it promises ere long to become the fashionable resort of those who have money to throw away, & who cannot be satisfied with the comfort which they find in their own houses.

One of the earliest builders of houses in the new seaside resort was, according to a story prevalent at the end of the century, a man by the name of Bakehouse. This was possibly Benjamin Backhouse, an Ipswich architect, surveyor, estate agent and builder who was busy in Ipswich and Bury St Edmunds between 1830 and 1870. The story goes that he built four houses on the cliff that were known for many years as Bakehouse's – or Backhouse's – Folly, since local people could not imagine that people would wish to occupy dwellings in such an exposed and lonely position.

By the time William White issued his *History, Gazetteer and Directory of Suffolk* in 1844, however, he was able to record that the village had been 'much improved of late years, by the erection of many neat houses for the accommodation of visitors, and it is now in high celebrity as a bathing place'. In the next edition of his directory in 1855, White recorded three bathing machine proprietors rather than just the one he had found 11 years earlier.

Perhaps the first to realise the attractions of Felixstowe was that extraordinary character Philip Thicknesse, patron of Thomas Gainsborough and Lieutenant-Governor of Landguard Fort from 1753 until he was relieved of that appointment in 1766. Thicknesse, who has been described as 'an unprincipled, eccentric, impetuous and curiously constituted being, possessing probably the worst temper that man was ever cursed with', purchased for his second wife a fisherman's cottage that nestled under the cliff, and this was extended into a very attractive seaside house known as Felixstowe Cottage. 'This retreat is now a handsome mansion, with beautiful grounds, and is occupied by J. C. Cobbold, Esq., of Ipswich, but belongs to Sir

Samuel Brudenell Fludyer, Bart.,' says William White in 1844. He added that the spring tides then approached within about 20 yards of the house, though in 1800 the pleasure grounds that lay between the house and the beach had extended for more than 200 yards.

John Chevallier Cobbold, Mayor of Ipswich in 1841, dock commissioner and prominent Ipswich businessman, not only had a seaside residence for the summer but built an hotel at Felixstowe in 1839. Already by that time a number of builders had erected 'neat houses and cottages which are let to visitors during the bathing season', and William Smith, licensee of the *Fludyer's Arms*, had become an owner not only of bathing machines but of a bath in which holidaymakers could soak themselves in salt water without the discomfort of having to enter the sea.

Walton as well as Felixstowe grew apace during the course of the century. While Felixstowe doubled its population between 1801 and 1841, Walton's population increased by a third in the same period, and it was only to be expected that when a Local Board was set up in 1887 it should cover both parishes. About the time that the Local Board came into being it was said that Walton as well as Felixstowe was much resorted to as a bathing place, and there were many good lodging-houses in the village, which still remained physically separated from its upstart, but still less populous, neighbour.

11. Tents on the beach in the 1880s, seen in one of Charles Emeny's early photographs. This was issued as a postcard in 1910 with the inscription 'Felixstowe 50 years ago'.

12. Developing Felixstowe, seen from the battery which fronted Q tower, in the early 1880s. The rough track curving down the cliff was named Convalescent Hill after the Suffolk Convalescent Home, seen on the left of this view. The leisure centre now occupies the site of the battery.

13.   George John Ward's shop on the corner of Hamilton Gardens and Ranelagh Road in 1869. Mr. Ward, who was a grocer and tea dealer as well as a draper, was one of the town's early businessmen, having the agency for W. & A. Gilbey, the wine and spirit merchants. The house on the Hamilton Gardens side has a balcony, later to become a typical feature of Felixstowe's architecture.

14. Carriages probably owned by James Moore, fly proprietor, at the bottom of Bent Hill, seen in a photograph taken by Charles Emeny in August 1877. The house on the corner, Bent Hill Cottage, later became the *Grand Hotel*, the licence being transferred from the old *Pig and Whistle*, a somewhat ancient hostelry on the corner of Maybush Lane and High Road East.

15. The *Pig and Whistle* at Old Felixstowe, one of the village's earlier places of refreshment. The licence was transferred to the *Grand Hotel* at the bottom of Bent Hill in the 1890s.

16. When Charles Emeny took this photograph *c.*1870 the *Fludyer's Arms* was a wooden building at the back of the beach. Built *c.*1833, it was replaced early in this century by a brick hotel built close alongside.

17. Looking across Landguard Common from Tower Hill, near Q tower, now known as South Hill, with the first houses in Sea Road under construction, almost hidden by a recently-built pair of houses in Undercliff Road. The picture is dated 1885. In the distance is tower P and the Manor House, and in the right distance is the railway station.

18. Another view from Tower Hill showing houses in Undercliff Road and, at extreme left, the first houses being erected in Sea Road. The Felixstowe Railway and Dock Company office can just be seen beyond the railway station. Some of the Undercliff Road houses survive but the wooden building nearest the camera has gone.

19. Buildings in Wolsey Gardens can be seen under construction in this view of the beach from the vicinity of the old battery in the 1880s. Convalescent Hill is still quite a rough roadway up the cliff.

20.   The corner of Wolsey Gardens and Victoria Parade, as the lower end of Hamilton Road was known. At no. 1 Victoria Parade was William Bennett, family grocer and provision merchant, who proudly recorded over his door that he had supplied the German Empress during her visit in 1891. The wooden building on the corner of Stanley Road, with windows looking out over the corner, is Eastward Ho College, a private school which prepared boys 'for Cambridge or Oxford, and for the Civil Service and other examinations'.

Colonel Tomline, the Railway and the Dock

The man who was largely responsible for the growth and development of modern Felixstowe was George Tomline, often known to his contemporaries as Colonel Tomline. Purchasing the Orwell Park estate at Nacton, some six miles west of Old Felixstowe, following the death of Sir Robert Harland in 1848, Tomline spent much time and money acquiring further land in Suffolk, and particularly in the area between Ipswich and Felixstowe. At the time of his death in 1889 it was said that he was the owner of the second largest estate in Suffolk, his holdings covering no less than 18,473 acres and being worth some £24,000 in rentals.

Tomline was a larger-than-life character, remembered in the area as an eccentric millionaire who made a hobby of litigation, even taking on the mighty War Office and winning his case. The facts of his life are rather different from the legend.

He was the son of William Edward Tomline, Esquire, of Riby Grove in Lincolnshire, and grandson of George Pretyman Tomline, Bishop of Winchester. The Pretyman family had held estates at Bacton and Old Newton in Suffolk since 1200.

As was natural for a gentleman of independent means in Victorian times, Tomline entered politics, becoming a Liberal M.P., but in spite of the ability he undoubtedly possessed he did not take his politics seriously. 'He is a sort of gentleman amateur in politics and in the discussion of public questions', said a contemporary in a somewhat dismissive comment on his work.

He was, indeed, something of an enigma to his contemporaries, who were quite unable to understand his complex character. He had no time for the ostentatious 'charity' beloved of many Victorians that did so little to solve the real problems of poverty and despair, but believed that it was the duty of wealthy landowners to provide employment for those less fortunate. Much of what he did on his Suffolk estates was based on this philosophy. Having settled at Orwell Park, he began acquiring land in the Colneis Hundred between Ipswich and Felixstowe and planning the development of his estate.

One of the first farms to be purchased was Wadgate Farm, Felixstowe, and that was followed by Peewit Farm, Old Hall Farm, East End Farm and Grange Farm at Felixstowe and others in neighbouring parishes. Then in 1867 Tomline took the opportunity to buy more than 6,000 acres that had belonged to the Duke of Hamilton; included in the purchase were six farms, the *Walton Ferry Inn* and about one thousand acres of shore and saltings. By the 1870s he owned a large part of the land on which the town of Felixstowe was to grow in subsequent years.

Tomline's vision was a new town that would be both a seaside resort and a port at the south end of Felixstowe, on the land that he owned. For the last 20 years of his life he devoted a great deal of energy to the realisation of his dream, and in the process he provided employment not just for those in his own pay but for many others who benefited indirectly from the schemes he undertook.

The first necessity was to provide a more ready means of access to Felixstowe from Ipswich and beyond. The road from Ipswich was a rough, poor one and the carriers' carts that used it were said to be so slow that passengers would walk on ahead to roadside hostelries, where they would refresh themselves and play the grand old game of three pins until the lumbering vehicles arrived outside. Hardly more expeditious than the carriers' carts was the horse-drawn omnibus operated by Samuel Fulcher that ran a daily service to and from Ipswich, whose hard seats were said to be quite ineffective in cushioning the jolts and jars as the iron-shod wheels dropped into the many ruts and potholes.

Various plans were drawn up for a tramway or railway to link Ipswich with the southern end of Felixstowe, where the colonel planned to build a new town that would cater for the thousands of people wanting to spend their summers by the sea. The line was intended to end on a pier projecting into Harwich harbour, from which steamers would ply to northern Germany.

Early plans were thwarted by the spirited opposition of Sir George Broke-Middleton, of Broke Hall, Nacton. Sir George complained that construction of the line would prevent sheep being driven from one part of his land to another, and also that it would cut the flight line of ducks to his decoy pond at Nacton. At last in 1875 a Felixstowe Railway and Pier Act was passed authorising the construction of a railway from Westerfield to Felixstowe; the line was to have its own station at Westerfield alongside the Great Eastern station, but it seems likely that there was a junction between the two lines from the beginning.

Construction of a single-line railway was entrusted to an East Anglian firm of civil engineers, Lucas Brothers of Lowestoft and Lambeth, and the work went ahead without delay. The choice of Westerfield as a terminus is most likely explained by the fact that Tomline was intending to build a further line right across Suffolk to link up with the Midland Railway near Cambridge, thus giving Felixstowe first-class connections with the industrial Midlands.

Tomline was able to see clearly that the future of Felixstowe as a port lay not with the Great Eastern Railway, whose continental steamers then ran from the other side of Harwich harbour and whose chairman, a gentleman named Parkes, was also chairman of the Victoria Docks and had no wish to see traffic leave the Thames for the Orwell; his name was later given to the new quay built in the River Stour for the G.E.R. steamer services.

A line from Westerfield to Chesterton Junction, a short distance north of Cambridge, was proposed in 1885 in a Felixstowe, Ipswich and Midlands Railway Bill. This would have linked with the Midland Railway, an important company that had an enormous coal trade but no outlet to the North Sea; had the link been made the Midland would certainly have promoted the development of the port of Felixstowe just as later it boosted Tilbury Docks, now a rival of Felixstowe. Just what was behind the failure of this Bill to make its way through Parliament is unclear, but the railway that might have brought so much trade to the port of Felixstowe joined the many railway projects that never reached the construction stage.

The railway from Westerfield to Felixstowe pier did open on 1 May 1877; a small 2-4-0 tank engine named *Tomline* hauled the first train with Tomline and his guests on board. Together with two other engines, named *Orwell* and *Felixstowe*, the *Tomline* operated the trains for two years until 1879, when an agreement was entered into by the Felixstowe Railway and Pier Company and the Great Eastern Railway Company for the latter to work the line. By then Tomline was involved with a further project – the construction of a dock that was, after many years, to become the germ of the modern port of Felixstowe.

The first plans for a dock were drawn up in 1875, but it was not until 1879, the year that the G.E.R. began working the Felixstowe line, that a Bill authorising the construction of a dock passed successfully through Parliament.

The contractors, Samuel Lake and Company, began work on digging out the dock basin towards the end of 1881. Only a year later the Felixstowe Railway and Dock Company, as it had been renamed after the passing of the 1879 Act, received notice that the contractors were insolvent and could not carry on with the work. The last monthly payment due to the contractors was used by Tomline to pay out the labourers, who besieged his agent's house on Landguard Common when the day came for them to receive their last wages.

It was not until the autumn of 1883 that a new contract was awarded to Henry Lee and work began again. As the navvies worked away with their spades and their barrows to excavate the basin, the quay on the south side of the dock was being constructed using huge concrete boxes that were sunk into the sand by digging out material from inside them. It was the Victorian engineer's way of providing firm foundation for a quay built on less than stable soil.

At least part of the quay was ready, but work on the rest of the project was by no means complete, when the first vessel, the little ss *Crathie*, a coasting tramp of 481 gross tons built of iron at Kinghorn in Scotland in 1884, arrived to unload a cargo of 471 tons of coal on 7 April 1886. The Railway and Dock Company paid £293 14s. for that cargo, which was doubtless sold locally; in later years the company distributed coal by sailing barge to customers at places such as Pin Mill and Levington. The little *Crathie* was to earn ignominy in 1895 when she collided with the German liner *Elbe* in the North Sea and disappeared into the fog; the *Elbe* sank with the loss of some 400 lives.

After the *Crathie* had unloaded her coal in the spring of 1886 it was three months before another vessel arrived in the dock. The barque *Prins Christian August* entered on 22 July with timber from the Norwegian port of Larvik, and she was followed three weeks later by the sailing barge *Alice* with 22 tons of cement. Almost certainly the cement had been brought from the Medway for use on the construction of the new quay or other work around the dock; earlier cargoes had been landed on the foreshore between the tides by similar spritsail barges.

By the end of the year the dock was quite busy, seven ships arriving with cargo in September and another nine in October, but all was not well with Tomline's enterprises. Indeed, it was to be much more than half a century before the dock fulfilled its early promise, and the scheme for linking Felixstowe with the Midlands by a cross-country railway line had failed to come to fruition. With the failure of this scheme Tomline was persuaded, much against his inclination, to sell the Westerfield to Felixstowe line to the Great Eastern in 1887. The man who negotiated the sale was Charles Cheston, a London solicitor who acted as Tomline's legal agent for several years. Cheston built himself a home in Felixstowe, and when he died in London in 1906 he was hailed as one of the pioneers of the town. It was then recorded that he did not continue as Tomline's agent for long after negotiating the sale of the railway, the inference being that Tomline was less than delighted with this action.

Tomline had complained of the Great Eastern that 'they starved us', and the sale of the line for £221,000, of which all but £57,000 was paid in G.E.R. stock, must have been a bitter pill for him to swallow. With the disposal of the line the company reversed its title, and ever afterwards was known as the Felixstowe Dock and Railway Company.

Whatever the Great Eastern Railway might do to promote the development of Felixstowe as a holiday resort, it continued to ensure that the dock did not rival its own establishment at Harwich and Parkeston Quay. By imposing unfair railway rates and by other means the company made certain that Felixstowe could not compete; at one stage the F.D.R.C. manager told the directors that 'for the provision of trucks we are entirely at the mercy of the G.E.R., who take care that we play second fiddle ...'.

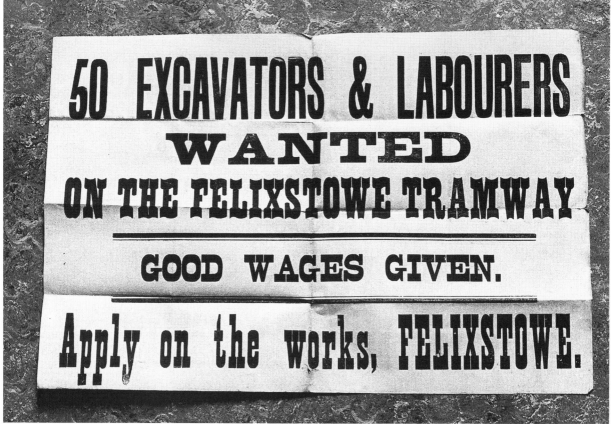

21. As a preliminary to his plans for the new town and port Colonel Tomline built a pier extending out into Harwich harbour in 1873 and laid a tramway from the pier across Landguard Common to near where the leisure centre stands today. This handbill offers good wages to those prepared to work on the construction of the tramway.

22. Colonel Tomline had three engines built by the Yorkshire Engine Company of Sheffield for the Felixstowe railway. This is No. 2, named *Orwell*, with one of the smart four-wheeled passenger coaches made for the line by the Gloucester Wagon Company, seen at Felixstowe station in May 1877, shortly after delivery.

23. Somewhat uncharacteristically, Colonel Tomline named engine No. 1 after himself. The engine is seen here at the head of a goods train, with its driver and other railway employees. When the purchase of rolling stock was authorised in February 1877, it was stated that the three engines cost £1,590 each; the first was to be delivered on the last day of April and the others in May that year.

24. The railway ran down on to the
pier, at the shore end of which was Pier
station. In the background can be seen
the *Pier Hotel*, built for the
accommodation of passengers using
the steamers that Tomline planned
should operate from the pier to
northern Germany. The continental
steamer service never materialised.

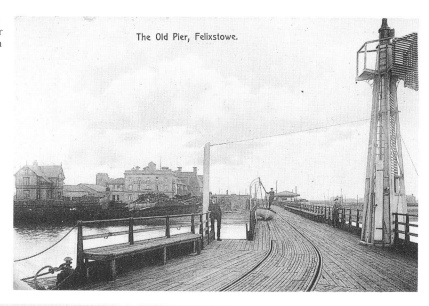

The Old Pier, Felixstowe.

25. One of the Great Eastern
Railway river steamers lying at
the pier in the 1890s.

26. A Great Eastern Railway
steamer approaches the pier at the
turn of the century. These three
steamers, the *Suffolk*, *Norfolk* and
Essex, ran from Ipswich to Harwich
and Felixstowe, continuing a
service inaugurated in 1850 by the
Eastern Union Railway.

27. Felixstowe station in 1883 after the working of the line had been taken over by the Great Eastern Railway. The train standing in the station is headed by G.E.R. No. 231, one of Massey Bromley's E10 class 0-4-4s, built at Stratford in 1880.

28. Work begins on the excavation of the dock, which Colonel Tomline planned as a gateway to the north of Europe. Excavations began in November 1881, but progress was slow and was held up entirely when the original contractor became insolvent the following year.

29. Sinking the caissons that formed the foundation of the quay within the dock. This unconventional method was used to ensure that the quay was firmly founded even though the underlying ground was mainly loose sand.

30.   Another view of the caissons showing the arrangement for extracting the spoil from within. In the background can be seen the *Pier Hotel* and a spritsail barge that is probably landing materials for the construction of the dock.

31 & 32.   For a period before the First World War the Shipbreaking Company Ltd. broke up iron ships in the dock and sent the scrap away by sea. Here the second-class cruiser HMS *Melampus*, built by Vickers in 1890, is being broken up in 1911. Three years earlier the old Royal Yacht *Osborne*, a wooden paddle steamer built at Pembroke Dock in 1870, had been broken up at Felixstowe.

Last Days of the Royal Yacht "Osborne"
Broken up at Felixstowe Docks. October. 1908
"We would not if we could - forget"   C. Kingsley.

33. The original offices of the Felixstowe Dock and Railway Company were housed in a timber building that was one of several in Felixstowe imported from Norway. The company records for 1888 contain an item 'Bugge and Co for Office building £200', but it would appear that the total cost of erection was considerably more than that. It is now a listed building.

34. The Manor House at the south end of Felixstowe seafront was part of Colonel Tomline's plan for the new town he intended to develop. Envisaged as an hotel when built in 1877, it was not successful as such and in 1883 Tomline adopted it as his home when in Felixstowe; the manor courts were held there annually. In this century it reverted to being an hotel after being used as a school and, during the First World War, as a naval officers' billet.

35. Nearby is Manor Terrace, a fine Victorian row of dwellings that is seen here in a photograph of *c.*1908. The terrace still stands.

Local Government

36. The chairman of the Walton and Felixstowe Local Board, Mr. Felix Cobbold, prepares to lay the foundation stone of the Town Hall on 13 January 1892. The building cost £1,800, the site having been given by Captain E. G. Pretyman, Colonel Tomline's heir, who performed the opening ceremony in September the same year. Until the building of the Town Hall, the Local Board occupied offices in Bulls Cliff, a large building on top of the cliff.

37.   The Town Hall can be seen in the middle of this view of Undercliff Road just before the turn of the century. Beside the Town Hall at the foot of Convalescent Hill is the Eastward Ho estate office, a small wooden building from which W. C. Archer handled the development of the area.

19th-Century Expansion

The arrival of the railway in 1877 gave a definite boost to the holiday trade. The original station was at the south end of the town, where Tomline had intended that his new town should grow, but some distance from the real focus of the town as it grew up around the early hotels. Following the purchase of the Felixstowe line in 1887 the Great Eastern Railway did its utmost to create a demand for holidays by the sea, building a new station nearer the centre of the town in 1898. With the opening of Felixstowe Town, as the new station was known, the wooden station at the south end of the town became Felixstowe Beach.

The reputation of Felixstowe as a seaside resort was greatly enhanced in 1891 when the German Empress came to stay at South Beach with five of her young sons while the emperor, a grandson of Queen Victoria, was on an official visit to Britain. The young princes were landed at the pier from the imperial yacht *Hohenzollern* on 7 July and were joined by their mother, who came from London by special train, some days later. In accordance with the expressed wishes of the empress the youngsters were left to enjoy their pranks on the beach without any special public notice, but her arrival at the station was watched by a large and enthusiastic crowd.

The town received further royal recognition of its attractions in 1895 when the Prince of Wales, later King Edward VII, paid a visit while taking part in a regatta organised by the Royal Harwich Yacht Club. In much later years Mrs. Wallis Simpson stayed none too happily in Felixstowe while awaiting hearing of her divorce petition at Ipswich, and it is often said that Edward VIII visited her at Beach House, though this seems extremely unlikely.

Felixstowe would never look back after the visit of the Empress of Germany. The town had been made fashionable, and nobody could ever look down upon the place or upon the seaside holiday when it was patronised by such exalted visitors. Many well-to-do people from Ipswich built fine houses in the new streets of the seaside town, not a few of them designed by T. W. Cotman, architect nephew of John Sell Cotman, a leading member of the Norwich School of Artists. It was left to the Ipswich & Suffolk Freehold Land Society, an organisation that had been set up in 1849 with the primary object of enabling working men to acquire the vote by means of the 40-shilling franchise, to provide homes for the working and middle classes. In 1884 the Freehold Land Society purchased an estate adjoining the grounds of the *Bath Hotel* and built 14 houses known as Ocean Terrace on part of the land; the remainder was disposed of to members in 18 allotments on which houses were later built.

Other similar schemes followed in succeeding years, nine 'villas' being built on land at the corner of Montague Road and Cobbold Road in 1885 and further development being carried out on another piece of land bought the following year. The Freehold Land Society's role in the development of Felixstowe was a quite significant one, for in the 1890s more land was purchased and further new roads laid out. At the same time new houses were built by the society in Walton on land bought from Captain E. G. Pretyman, Colonel Tomline's heir and successor.

At this stage the town showed signs of growth, but it also showed signs of being raw and new. The church of St John the Baptist, on the site of the old battery, was a temporary structure of corrugated iron, and so was the Wesleyan Methodist chapel in Orwell Road; the Evangelical Free Church was no more than a small wooden building. Within a few years this was to change, for a fine new red brick church of St John the Baptist was built in Orwell Road in 1894-95, and the temporary structures occupied by the Free Churches also gave way to fine permanent buildings in the course of the following 10 years. Another temporary church, St Andrew's, was opened in 1907 near the Town station as a chapel of ease to the old parish church; St John the Baptist's had become a separate parish for the south end of the town on completion of the permanent church, and in 1912 the Roman Catholic community began the building of St Felix's church in Gainsborough Road, not very far from St Andrew's.

The new churches catered not only for an increasing resident population but also for a migrant summer population for which big new hotels were built around the turn of the century. In 1892 none of the town's hotels was of any size, the *Fludyer's Arms* being no more than a wooden building standing almost in isolation at the back of the beach, but in 1898 the *Orwell Hotel* opened in close proximity to the Town station, followed by the towering *Cliff Hotel* in 1906. Biggest and grandest of all was the *Felix Hotel*, designed by the Hon. Douglas Tollemache and T. W. Cotman, which opened in 1903 after having taken some three years to build. Its gardens extended to the top of the cliff.

Acquisition of the *Felix Hotel* by the Great Eastern in 1919 was a logical progression for that company, which had set out to do all that it could to develop Felixstowe as a seaside resort. In 1904 the company ran a two-and-a-half-hour non-stop service from Liverpool Street to Felixstowe, though the following year a stop was introduced at Westerfield so that the train could go on to Lowestoft after detaching a through Felixstowe portion. The down Lowestoft train was allowed a mere two minutes at Westerfield, and the Felixstowe coaches were timed to leave Westerfield only three minutes after the departure of the Lowestoft section, necessitating some very smart work indeed.

Bank holiday weekends were no holiday for workers on the Felixstowe branch in the early years of this century, for day trippers and holidaymakers came to the town in their thousands by train and boat. On August Monday the railway company operated a shuttle service between Derby Road station, to which passengers were taken by the electric trams which came into service in Ipswich in 1903, and the two main stations at Felixstowe. By 1912 the number of passengers travelling by train to Felixstowe had increased to the extent that at August holiday weekend more than 7,000 travelled from Liverpool Street to Felixstowe in four days, Thursday to Sunday, and on the Monday another 5,500 came down from London to join the 4,500 day trippers making the shorter journey from Derby Road. In addition nearly 3,500 passengers travelled downriver by the railway company's paddle steamers *Essex*, *Suffolk* and *Norfolk* from boat landing stages in the New Cut at Ipswich.

By this time holidaymakers could also come to Felixstowe by sea, for in 1905 the Coast Development Corporation opened a new pier reaching out more than 900 yards from Undercliff Road at which its Belle steamers berthed. The first vessel to moor to the pier in July 1905 was the *Woolwich Belle*, on her way from Ipswich to Clacton and Walton. Earlier the Belle steamers had been calling at Colonel Tomline's old pier at the south end of Felixstowe, which was in Great Eastern hands; and as the railway company ran their own steamers from that pier to Harwich and Ipswich they were no more co-operative with the Belle steamers than they were with the Dock and Railway Company. The steamers embarked and disembarked no fewer than 62,800 passengers at the new pier in 1926, in which year a large dance pavilion was opened at the shore end.

38.   By the *Fludyer's Arms* there were a number of groynes built to counter erosion, which had exposed large sections of underlying septaria. In this picture, taken in 1890, tower R can be seen on the site now occupied by the Bartlet Convalescent Home.

39. Edwardian children loved donkey-riding along the seafront. Here Doris Smith (in the middle), with her sister, Winifred, and their nursemaid, Ellen (on the right), and her cousin, Marjorie Hanson (on the left), pose for the photographer at the bottom of Bent Hill.

40. Two youngsters lean on the paled fence as they gaze down at the bathing huts which line the back of the beach. Behind them is the *Felix Hotel*, opened for only a short time when this photograh was taken. The cliff is still covered with rough turf and bushes.

41. By 1910 the cliff had been turned into gardens and the old rough paths down the cliff had been made into steps. *Quilter's Cliff Hotel* had been built in 1906, and some fine houses were being built along Hamilton Gardens; scaffolding surrounds one of them in this view.

42. The *Felix Hotel*, opened in 1903 by the Hon. Douglas Tollemache, boasted not only 250 bedrooms but also 20 grass tennis courts, eight hard courts, two full-size croquet lawns and an 18-hole putting course. In 1919 it was acquired by the Great Eastern Railway, which was energetically promoting the town as a holiday resort, and this aerial photograph was taken not long afterwards.

43. A view of Harvest House, formerly known as the *Felix Hotel*, through one of the wrought-iron garden gates. It has now been converted into flats after many years as offices.

44. The *Felix Hotel* can also be seen in this view of the gardens laid out on the cliffs. The tamarisk bushes said to have been first introduced by Philip Thicknesse grow in profusion here.

45. Holidaymakers stroll along the Promenade, *c.*1907. Some two miles in length, the Promenade and the granite sea wall were built by Felixstowe and Walton U.D.C. in 1902 at a cost of £36,000 to halt erosion which was threatening the *Fludyer's Arms* and other buildings close to the sea. On the left can be seen houses built in various materials and designs in Undercliff Road in late Victorian years.

46. Well wrapped up against the sea breezes, four youngsters pose for the photographer outside Mount Ridley, which with Hale Cottage forms one of the pairs of houses in Undercliff road just west of the bottom of Bent Hill. These are of timber construction, but other apartment houses nearer Bent Hill, though of basically similar appearance, are solidly built of brick.

The Town Station

47. Laying the loop that enabled trains to travel on to Beach and Pier stations after reversing in the new station when it was opened in 1898. On the left is the original line from Ipswich, the north curve, taken up after the opening of the Town station but reinstated in 1980 for the benefit of the increasing freight traffic to and from the dock.

48. An 'up' train leaving the Town station just a year after its opening. In the left foreground the signalman can be seen holding the tablet that gives the driver authority to enter the single-line section to Trimley, where a further tablet will authorise him to travel on to Derby Road. Beyond the train can be seen the *Orwell Hotel*, opened at the same time as the Town station.

49.   Passengers arriving at the Town station on 2 August 1899. The engine has run tender-first from Westerfield or Derby Road; on bank holiday weekends a shuttle service was operated from Derby Road for the benefit of day-trippers from Ipswich, and there was no turntable at that station.

The New Pier

50. In 1905 the Coast Development Corporation opened the new pier near the bottom of South Hill in connection with its steamer services between London and the east coast resorts. The first vessel to moor to the head of the 2,640-ft. pier, in July 1905, was the paddle steamer *Woolwich Belle*, which operated a service between Ipswich, Walton-on-Naze and Clacton.

51. The paddle steamer *London Belle*, biggest of the Belle steamers, approaching Felixstowe pier. The well-polished bell on the pierhead was rung to indicate to intending passengers that the steamer was about to depart. The *London Belle*, built by Denny Brothers at Dumbarton on the Clyde in 1893, served in the First World War as a minesweeper out of Harwich and then was converted into a hospital ship for service in the White Sea.

52. To carry passengers along the length of the pier an electric tramway of 3 ft. 6 in. gauge was provided; electricity was taken from the Felixstowe U.D.C. supply. Before the 1914-18 war the fare was a penny each way, but weekly, fortnightly and monthly tickets could be obtained; a full year's travel cost 10s. 6d. In this well-known view the three toast rack cars are running as a multiple unit – no passing loop was provided on the tramway. Holding on to his Panama hat is Clement Emeny, younger son of Charles Emeny, who took over his father's photographic business in Walton High Street. The three original cars were scrapped in 1931 and replaced by one mounted on the four-wheel truck of a former Ipswich tram. Above the roof of the tramcar can be seen tower Q, one of the martello towers, now hidden from view by surrounding buildings.

53. The pier can be seen in the background of this photograph of goat carts for hire on the Promenade in Edwardian times. Such carts were not confined to Felixstowe during this period, for Lowestoft and other similar resorts adopted goat carts for the amusement of juvenile Edwardians.

The Spa and the Hotels

54. Swiss Cottage was one of the early wooden houses built at the Spa end of the town on land bought by John Chevallier Cobbold from the Duke of Hamilton. Pipes were laid in the cliffs to collect water to supply the group of houses built by Cobbold; an early tap survives at the edge of the pavement.

55. A close-up of the tap in front of Swiss Cottage, relic of a 19th-century water supply scheme.

56. One of the advantages of Felixstowe as a resort was the presence of a natural spring, the water of which 'eminent physicians have said that in its aerated state it is an anti-dyspeptic and anti-gout water'. It was said to make 'a capital medicine for those suffering from nervous prostration, depression, and overwork'. A small pumphouse was built to provide the water, and a bandstand was erected nearby *c.*1907.

57. The Spa Pavilion, which had seating for more than 600 people in its original form, was designed in 1908 by the local council's surveyor, Harry Clegg, and was built by Harry J. Linzell, a builder with premises in Orwell Road; it incorporated the bandstand, which was enclosed with large windows. Linzell, who also had business interests in Ipswich and Newmarket, was one of the early telephone users in Felixstowe; his National Telephone number was 31.

58. The opening of the Spa Pavilion on 25 June 1909, by Lord Claud Hamilton, chairman of the Great Eastern Railway. He had been greeted on his arrival at the Town station by the chairman of the urban council, Mr. E. H. Woodmancy, who in his other position as secretary of the Felixstowe Dock and Railway Company had little cause to be grateful to the railway company.

59.   One of the earliest municipal facilities to be provided for the holidaymaker was the cliff shelter, erected in 1899 at a cost to the urban district council of £2,759. Set into the cliff between Bent Hill and Convalescent Hill, it contained a tea room and public conveniences.

60.   The *Grand Hotel* with its elaborate balcony came into being around the turn of the century to cater for the increasing number of visitors seeking the kind of accommodation offered by an hotel. Earlier visitors staying in the town for an extended period had preferred to rent whole houses or to stay in apartment houses.

61. On Bent Hill behind the *Grand Hotel* were refreshment and dining rooms operated in conjunction with that establishment. This photograph of *c*.1905 also shows shops on the corner of Hamilton Road and Hamilton Gardens.

62.   An advertisement for the *Bath Hotel*, which had developed from the original hotel built by J. C. Cobbold in 1839. It appeared in *Pictures of East Coast Health Resorts*, a turn-of-the-century publication that promoted the rising seaside towns from Clacton to the Wash.

63. The *Cliff Hotel*, built in 1906 for George Robert Quilter and Miss Quilter, was quite new when this photograph was taken. Before having the *Cliff Hotel* designed for them by Henry William Buxton, an architect who was responsible for many other buildings in Felixstowe, the Quilters had been at the *Bath Hotel* for almost a quarter of a century. Their father, Henry George Quilter, had come from Aston, Birmingham, to take over the *Bath Hotel*.

64. The *Cliff Hotel* lost its iron balconies during the scrap-metal drives of the Second World War and was later converted to offices. Today, renamed Cliff House, it remains in office use and sports a radar aerial, part of the Harwich Haven Authority's radar system covering the harbour approaches.

65.   Somewhat over-dressed for the beach by present-day standards, Edwardian youngsters nevertheless managed to enjoy themselves, even if there was a shortage of sand for the making of sandcastles; Felixstowe beach is largely composed of pebbles.

66. Hamilton Road, which became the town's main shopping street, is the main route from Felixstowe Town station, opened in 1898, to the seafront. The southern end, shown here, was at the beginning of this century still known as Victoria Parade; when this photograph was taken *c.*1907 Miss Jessie Wall, stationer, was at no. 8. Opposite at no. 11, next to the post office, was fancy draper Frank Mason, who also had a much larger establishment on the corner of Tavern Street and Tower Street, Ipswich.

67.   This view of Hamilton Road *c.*1912 shows the quite pretentious buildings that by then lined the southern end of the road. The Y.W.C.A., whose premises can be seen above the florist's shop of Surman and Surman, also had a holiday home in Leopold Road at this time.

The Churches

68. The earliest of the town's Nonconformist churches was this wooden building in Ranelagh Road, erected at a cost of £160 and opened in 1869 as Felixstowe Evangelical Free Church. Although its place was taken in 1898 by a new Congregational church in the same road, it survived until this century, and was then used as a store by a local electrical goods manufacturer.

69. The church of SS. Peter and Paul, Felixstowe, as it was *c*.1840 before the Victorian restoration and the addition of transepts and a new chancel. The stump of the tower and other parts of the church are built of septaria, the cement stone which in the early 19th century was dredged off Felixstowe for the roman cement industry.

70. Old Felixstowe church after the building of the transepts and chancel in 1876.

71. The church of St Mary at Walton, *c.*1914. Some fifty years earlier it had been described as 'much injured by time, having lost its once fine tower, the west end of the nave, and part of the chancel', but subsequent restoration gave it back what it had lost, and a south aisle in addition. A rather squat new tower was added in 1899.

72. The temporary church of St Andrew, opened as a daughter church of Old Felixstowe church in 1907, was built by John Harrison and Company, of Camberwell, London. It was intended to serve the expanding area around the Town station, and had seating for about four hundred people.

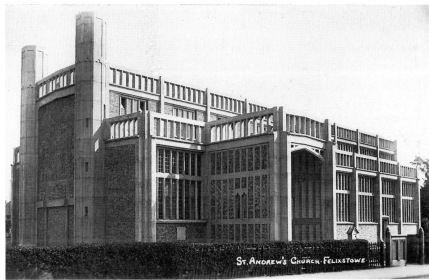

73. Concrete is an uncompromising material and does not weather with age, but the new church of St Andrew built in St Andrew's Road in 1929-30 was intended by its architects, Hilda Mason and Raymond Erith, to be a modern reflection of Suffolk church-building traditions. Its starkness is now masked by trees, but the tower that was part of the original design has yet to be added.

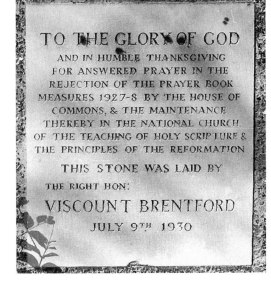

TO THE GLORY OF GOD
AND IN HUMBLE THANKSGIVING
FOR ANSWERED PRAYER IN THE
REJECTION OF THE PRAYER BOOK
MEASURES 1927-8 BY THE HOUSE OF
COMMONS, & THE MAINTENANCE
THEREBY IN THE NATIONAL CHURCH
OF THE TEACHING OF HOLY SCRIPTURE &
THE PRINCIPLES OF THE REFORMATION

THIS STONE WAS LAID BY
THE RIGHT HON:
VISCOUNT BRENTFORD
JULY 9TH 1930

74. The foundation stone of St Andrew's church reveals the source of the money for its building and also the reason for it being given.

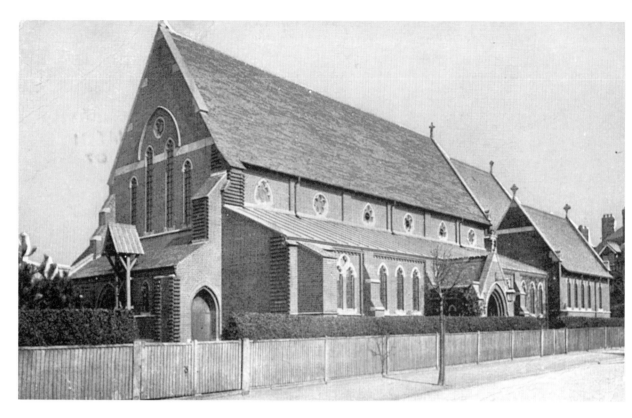

75 & 76. St John's church in Orwell Road became the centre of a new parish serving the south end of the town on its completion in 1895. The design by Sir Arthur Blomfield and Son provided for the later construction of a tower, as can be seen from the brickwork at the south-west corner. The picture below shows it in the 1920s after the addition of the tower and spire, and shows also the Calvary erected in the churchyard in 1920 as a memorial to men of the parish who died in the First World War.

Felixstowe in the 20th Century

77.   The Picture Playhouse on the corner of Hamilton Road and York Road was built in 1914 by Walter Cross, a Felixstowe builder, to the designs of Colonel Harold Ridley Hooper, of Ipswich. The original plans included a lock-up shop and, on the first floor, a tea lounge; a revision of the plans replaced the shop with an office and the tea-room with a promenade lounge. The building was demolished in 1970 when the site was redeveloped.

78.   The model yacht pond, seen here in the early 1920s, was a popular facility for very many years. The old Pier Pavilion on the right of the picture advertises the White Coons, who under Mr. Ben Lawes were most popular entertainers in Felixstowe between 1910 and 1921.

79.   When it first opened in 1868 the Suffolk Convalescent Home at the bottom of what became known as Convalescent Hill was a wooden building intended for the accommodation of small numbers of patients. The first extension, with the two dormers to the right of the picture, was built in 1885; it is seen here *c.*1912, with the urban council's water cart standing in front.

80.   Sea Road, towards the south end of the town, would have provided the seafront of George Tomline's proposed seaside resort. In this turn-of-the-century view Q tower can be seen on the cliff; South Hill has not yet been laid out.

81. An aerial photograph by Emeny of Sea Road and the model yacht pond. Q tower can be seen on the right, and just beyond it the tower of St John's church is under construction, dating the photograph to 1913-14. The railway line to Beach station is visible to the upper left.

The Bath Hotel Fire

82. The *Bath Hotel*, Felixstowe's first hotel, had at one time been known as the *Hamilton Arms*; much of the land in the area had been owned by the Duke of Hamilton until sold in 1867. It was said that the original part of the hotel had been built from the bricks of tower S, a martello tower at the north end of Felixstowe that was pulled down in the 1830s when it became unsafe. Because of the seasonal nature of the holiday trade, the hotel was still closed on 28 April 1914 when two militant suffragettes, Hilda Burkett and Florence Tunks, set fire to the building to draw attention to the campaign for votes for women. The fire was first noticed by coastguards at P tower and by the crew of the Cork lightship soon after 4 a.m., and the flames spread with remarkable rapidity, or as one onlooker put it, 'like a rat scuttling along the floor'.

83. Hampered by a lack of water pressure, the 16 men of the U.D.C.'s fire brigade under Superintendent William Burchell and Captain Denis Cowles were unable to prevent the flames from destroying much of the hotel, seen here boarded up following the fire.

84. Within eight minutes of receiving warning of the fire, William Burchell had sounded the 'hooter' to call the brigade and had set off with the brigade's handcart, seen here manned by six of the firemen. Most of the part-time firemen were employed in the building trade, which was said to give them useful knowledge of building construction.

85. In 1903 the brigade had taken delivery of a Shand, Mason steam fire engine, seen here in the yard of the fire station in Hamilton Road.

86. The two suffragettes gained entry to the hotel by way of the kitchen window, found still open after the fire had been put out.

87. A large and not entirely friendly crowd assembled outside the Town Hall when Birkett and Tunks arrived from
Ipswich prison for the committal proceedings in May 1914. Extra police had been drafted into the town in case of trouble;
their main role seems to have been merely to clear a path to the door for the two defendants.

Serving the Sick

88.   The Croydon Cottage Hospital was built in Constable Road in 1909 to serve Felixstowe and Walton. Both the site and the building itself were given by Mr. C. H. E. Croydon, an Ipswich jeweller who had a home in Montague Road, Felixstowe, and the building was erected by Thomas Ward and Son, one of the oldest building firms in the district. As seen here it had only 10 beds, but in 1920 it was enlarged and given another 18 beds, the cost being met by the surplus of funds raised for canteens in the town during the 1914-18 war and for the war memorial.

89.   The surviving part of the *Bath Hotel*, on the left, became a nurses' home for a convalescent home in the 1920s. Named after J. H. Bartlet, who died in 1917 leaving money for the purpose of setting up a convalescent home in connection with the East Suffolk and Ipswich Hospital, the Bartlet Convalescent Home was opened in 1926. It covers the site of tower R, one of the chain of martello towers, the foundations of which are said to be incorporated into the building. This photograph shows the home at around the time it opened.

90. The Bartlet Convalescent Home seen from the beach. The white weatherboarded building at the back of the beach on the left is the former *Bath Hotel Tap*, which by the 1920s had become Mrs. Matilda Grayston's refreshment rooms.

Felixstowe Ferry

91. Felixstowe Golf Club was founded in 1880, and by 1892 it had nearly 500 members. The clubhouse shown here had formerly been the farmhouse of East End Farm.

92. The golf links looking back towards the town. The clubhouse can be seen in the distance on the right; the building in the foreground was reserved for lady members.

93. Tower U, then in use by the coastguard, and the little corrugated iron church of St Nicholas at Felixstowe Ferry at the beginning of this century. Opened as a mission church by the vicar of Felixstowe c.1889, St Nicholas' church was wrecked by a bomb that fell nearby in 1943, and was replaced just over ten years later by a new building of about the same size.

94. Felixstowe Ferry was already the resort of weekend motorists when this picture was taken c.1910. The hut in the middle advertises teas, which were served by a member of the Newson family. Its place was taken many years later by the Ferry Café.

95. A view of Felixstowe Ferry c.1910 with one of Sir Cuthbert Quilter's steam ferries crossing the Deben. In the background is Bawdsey Manor, the first part of which was built by Sir Cuthbert in 1886; further sections were added over the next 20 years, the final part being the White Tower seen to the left of the building, which was finished by 1905. Local legend has it that Sir Cuthbert, a stockbroker, added a tower for each million he added to his fortune.

96. A spritsail barge lying at anchor in the Deben at Felixstowe Ferry in the early years of the century. Such craft traded regularly to the cement factory at Waldringfield as well as to the port of Woodbridge.

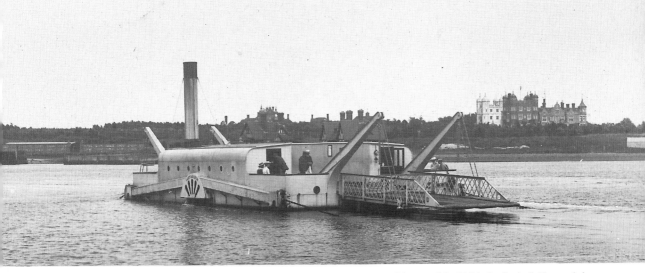

97.   The steam ferry *Lady Quilter* crossing the Deben towards Bawdsey. Built at Plymouth in 1894, the *Lady Quilter* and the smaller *Lady Beatrice* operated the ferry until laid up in 1931 and later scrapped. The steam machinery wound in a chain laid from shore to shore, propelling the ferries across the river. Sir Cuthbert Quilter died in 1911, at about the time this photograph was taken.

98.   A car being driven ashore from the ferry *Lady Beatrice*, *c*.1908. The chain by which the ferry hauled itself across the river can be clearly seen in the foreground.

Trades and Industries

99.   The smock mill at Walton, in a picture taken in the 1860s by Richard Dykes Alexander, an Ipswich businessman and pioneer amateur photographer who had a summer home at Lavender Cottage, Walton. With its two pairs of patent self-regulating sails and fantail winding, Walton Mill was then a thoroughly up-to-date windmill. The tower of the mill is still to be seen just to the south of Walton High Street.

100.   The development of the town towards the end of Victoria's reign led to a considerable demand for bricks, supplied in part from the local brickworks operated by Bugg and Jolly. Here the brickmakers worked in the open with only rough shelters to protect them from the sun and the rain; that on the left has a straw-covered hurdle forming part of the roof. Firing of the bricks is in progress; in the background smoke pours from the top of a typical updraught kiln.

101. Many men found employment as bricklayers and carpenters when the building trade was booming in the town.
These men are at work on the stables of The Lodge, designed by T. W. Cotman in 1900 for Felix Thornley Cobbold and
built the following year. The bearded man standing in the front row is foreman bricklayer Fred Studd. The Lodge later
became known as Cobbold's Point and was in 1929 taken over by Felixstowe Ladies' College, a public school for girls set
up under the Stowe and Canford Trust. More than 60 years later it is just one of the boarding houses of Felixstowe College,
as it is now known.

102. Staff of the International Tea Company's store at 6 Victoria Parade in the early years of the century. The International Stores occupied this site for many years, having moved in when the shops at the southern end of Hamilton Road were built in the 1880s. In this century the firm also had a branch at 262 High Street.

103. Before the coming of the internal combustion engine, horses were used by tradesmen of all kinds for deliveries and cartage. Newly set up in business at Trimley St Martin and delivering his bread and confectionery all over the Felixstowe area, William Cooper posed on his horse-drawn delivery cart, c.1909. His hygienic bakery at Trimley St Martin seems not to have survived all that long; perhaps he went to war and never returned, for in 1916 the business was operated by the Misses Rhoda and Rachel Cooper, possibly his daughters.

104. This group of workers is at the gas-works near Beach station operated by the Felixstowe Gas and Light Company, which placed regular contracts for Yorkshire coal to be landed at the dock and carted to the works in Walton Avenue. There was a considerable local trade in coke and other by-products of gas production until the closure of the works in 1931, after which gas was brought by main from the Ipswich Gas Light Company's works at Ipswich.

105. William G. Clarke was in business as a jobmaster in the eastern part of Beach Road in the 1890s, and he continued to be listed in directories as a jobmaster until the last Suffolk *Kelly's* came out in 1937, although, as can be seen in this pre-1914 photograph, he had espoused the cause of the horseless carriage from an early day. When this photograph was taken the further building still advertised Clarke's Livery Stables and another advertisement offered pony traps for hire, but the nearer building is labelled 'Garage' and offers cars for hire.

106. Another early garage in the town was that on the corner of Hamilton Road and Cobbold Road belonging to Robert William Pratt, who was able to offer 'Pratt's Perfection Spirit' with a proprietorial air; in fact Pratt's spirit took its name from Charles Pratt, an American oil refiner and an associate of John D. Rockefeller.

PRATT'S GARAGE

Telephone 45.

THE A A GARAGE

*Excellent Accommodation for Cars,
Cars for Hire.
Repairs, Accessories, Oil, &c., &c.*

HAMILTON ROAD,

FELIXSTOWE

107. An advertisement from the *Suffolk County Handbook* for Pratt's Garage, which was declared to be 'The A.A. Garage'.

Felixstowe at War

During the period of the Revolutionary and Napoleonic Wars with France there were very real fears of an invading army landing on the English coast, and plans were made to counter this threat. In 1797 Major-General John Moore, better known as Sir John Moore, the hero of Corunna, made a survey of the Essex and Suffolk coast to determine the measures needed to repel an invading army, and then in 1808 there began the construction of a chain of towers from the mouth of the River Colne to near Aldeburgh.

Eight of these martello towers were built along the Felixstowe shore between Harwich harbour and the Deben, two others being placed on the Shotley peninsula. Tower N – all east coast towers were known by a letter of the alphabet – stood at Walton Ferry and like several others had a large battery in front of it. These towers, which mounted three guns on the roof of each as well as those in the batteries, were ovoid in plan with the point facing the sea.

Four of the Felixstowe towers have disappeared: the site of tower N and the 'Dooley Fort' lies beneath the dock complex, tower O on Landguard Point was washed away many years ago, tower R was demolished before the building of the Bartlet Convalescent Home, and tower S further to the north was abandoned as early as 1835 as unsafe. The others remain.

Felixstowe enjoyed a military presence during the 19th and early 20th centuries not only through the Royal Garrison Artillery at Landguard Fort, but from time to time through the holding of Volunteer and Territorial camps on Landguard Common. The Territorial Battalion of the Gloucestershire Regiment received new colours while in camp on the Common in 1913.

Landguard Fort not only had its regular garrison of Royal Garrison Artillery but was also manned from time to time by members of the Territorial Army who came for their annual training. At the beginning of this century Felixstowe had its own company of Royal Garrison Artillery Volunteers who became part of the Territorial Army on its formation in 1906.

In June 1913, Ipswich Territorials were in Landguard Fort while the Harwich and Felixstowe Territorials manned Beacon Hill Fort on the other side of the harbour for an exercise involving naval vessels that attempted to gain entrance during the night. Thanks to the work of the Fortress Company, Royal Engineers from Chelmsford who manned the searchlights, the 'attackers' were driven off, but in the course of the night two destroyers, HMS *Lively* and HMS *Violet*, collided just outside the harbour, sustaining damage that forced them to go to Sheerness for repairs.

In that same year the Committee of Imperial Defence recommended the construction of a new fort, at the north end of the town, to cover an area that could not be covered by the guns at Landguard Fort and in Beacon Hill Fort on the Harwich side of the harbour. The new fort was named after General Brackenbury, the Director of Army Intelligence. Two 9.2-inch guns, the most powerful weapons ever to be mounted on the east coast, were emplaced there in 1915, and until the fort became operational a 9.2-inch railway gun was brought into use on a railway spur constructed from the sidings at the Town station towards the fort.

Harwich harbour had been a naval base for centuries, and Felixstowe became much involved in naval matters when in 1908 an oil fuel barge was moored in the dock to provide bunkering facilities for destroyers based in the harbour. The destroyer moorings were on the Felixstowe side, just above the dock. Later two 2,500-ton oil tanks were erected at the back of the dock to store oil fuel for the Admiralty, and the coming and going of naval vessels greatly enlivened the scene at the dock.

About the same time, one of the martello towers, tower P at the south end of the town, became the site of a naval radio station, a large mast being erected to support the necessary aerials. This station acquired particular importance when war broke out in 1914 and naval forces operating from Harwich became active in the North Sea, sinking the German minelayer *Konigin Luise* within 12 hours of the declaration of war.

Felixstowe was crowded with visitors on August Monday, 1914, a bank holiday that was overshadowed by the threat of war. When Britain's ultimatum to Germany expired, the holidaymakers left in a rush, and within the week the town was virtually under military control; a yachtsman who entered the dock at that time was met by a sentry with fixed bayonet who refused to allow him ashore.

During the First World War Felixstowe was attacked from the air twice, not by zeppelins but by formations of bombers operating from airfields in Belgium. Altogether 30 people were killed in the two raids, the majority of them servicemen; the air station and premises being used as army billets were hit in both attacks, and one flying boat was destroyed and another badly damaged in the first raid, on 4 July 1917.

108. The Suffolk Artillery Brigade Militia taking part in a sham fight on Landguard Common in 1854, in a painting by John Duvall. Landguard Fort, still largely as built in 1749, can be seen on the left.

109. P tower, then in the hands of HM Coastguard, dressed overall for the celebrations of Queen Victoria's birthday, 24 May 1900. The Coastguard was in those days controlled by the Admiralty and formed a naval reserve; the tower remained in use by the Coastguard when this organisation was taken over by the Board of Trade in 1924, and has in recent years been the local headquarters of the Royal Naval Auxiliary Service as well as having the Coastguard lookout perched on the roof.

110. The band of No. 3 Company (Felixstowe) of the 1st Suffolk and Harwich Royal Garrison Artillery Volunteers. The bandsmen all wear the Broderick, a form of cap that had a fairly short life in the army; later, as No. 6 Company of the Essex and Suffolk Royal Garrison Artillery, Territorial Army, they wore spiked helmets. The Felixstowe company, which in 1913 had an authorised establishment of three officers and 60 N.C.O.s and men, sometimes marched from its drill hall in Garrison Lane to St John's church, led by the band.

111. Brackenbury Fort from the air in its last days when only Brackenbury Barracks, on the other side of the road, was in use. The emplacements for the two 9.2-in. guns can be seen, together with the shallow ditch and iron fence that surrounded the battery. An earthen parapet gives some protection from the rear to the two gun positions, which had magazines and shelters beneath them. Below the cliff are two searchlight positions added in 1941 to give the battery the capacity to operate at night. The fort was demolished by Felixstowe U.D.C. in 1969, though not without great difficulty.

112. Some of the defences constructed in the Felixstowe area during the First World War can be seen in this photograph of the beach in front of Sea Road. A platoon of soldiers, rifles at the slope, is marching along the promenade. Many of the hotels and larger houses in the town had been commandeered as military billets, and some of the town's leading businessmen had to find themselves other accommodation when their homes were requisitioned.

113.   Considerable damage was done in the town in two air raids by Gotha bombers flying from bases in Belgium in July 1917. The second raid occurred just after 8 o'clock on a Sunday morning, 22 July, while worshippers were at communion in Old Felixstowe church; the parson paused for a moment as bombs exploded nearby, glanced at the congregation, then carried on with the service.

114.   One of the bombs dropped on the stables at the back of the *Ordnance Hotel*. One of those killed in the raid was a waiter who was standing outside the hotel when the bombs exploded; other casualties included servicemen whose billets were hit.

115.   River-class destroyers steaming into harbour in 1913. Although officially based at Harwich, the destroyers had permanent moorings on the Felixstowe side of the harbour and used the dock for bunkering, oil fuel tanks having been installed in 1911 for bunkering the Navy's first oil-burning ships.

116.   Field Marshal Lord Allenby, who as commander-in-chief of the Egyptian Expeditionary Force had considerable success in a capmpaign against the Turks in 1917-18 and won a resounding victory at Megiddo in the latter year, was a member of a family well-known in Felixstowe. He had already been raised to the peerage as Viscount Allenby of Megiddo and Felixstowe in 1919 when given this enthusiastic reception on his return to the town.

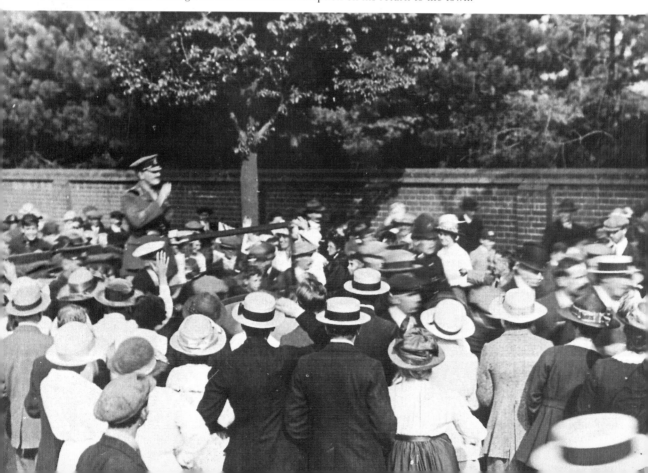

117. Lord Allenby unveiling the war memorial at Kirton.

The Second World War

Much more serious were the air raids that occurred during the Second World War, when Felixstowe again became something of an armed camp with two 12-inch railway guns of No. 9 Super Heavy Battery, Royal Artillery, operating from sidings alongside the Ipswich to Felixstowe line. Boom defence vessels based in the dock laid a boom across the entrance to Harwich harbour, and at the beginning of 1940 the depot ship HMS *Vulcan* and the 1st Motor Torpedo Boat Flotilla took up residence in the dock. Before long HMS *Beehive*, a Light Coastal Forces base, was in being, the dock was full of small warships, and the hangars of the R.A.F. station were taken over by the shipwrights who kept them in fighting fettle.

On 21 November 1939, the destroyer HMS *Gipsy* was sunk by a magnetic mine laid by a German naval seaplane between the air station and Landguard Fort as she was leaving harbour in the company of two other similar craft, one of them a Polish ship. It was a serious disaster causing severe loss of life; those who died, including the captain, were buried in the naval cemetery at Shotley.

It is said that at one stage there were no fewer than 2,000 naval personnel, 3,500 army personnel and 2,000 R.A.F. officers and men in and around Felixstowe. Anti-aircraft guns were set up in the area, the A.A. operations room being first at Landguard Fort and later at Q tower, one of the martello towers.

At the end of the war Felixstowe was faced with an enormous task in restoring the seafront, the hotels and the attractions which brought holidaymakers to the town. The pier, breached in 1940 by Royal Engineers, was left in its truncated state, only the pavilion at the shore end being put back into something like its pre-war state.

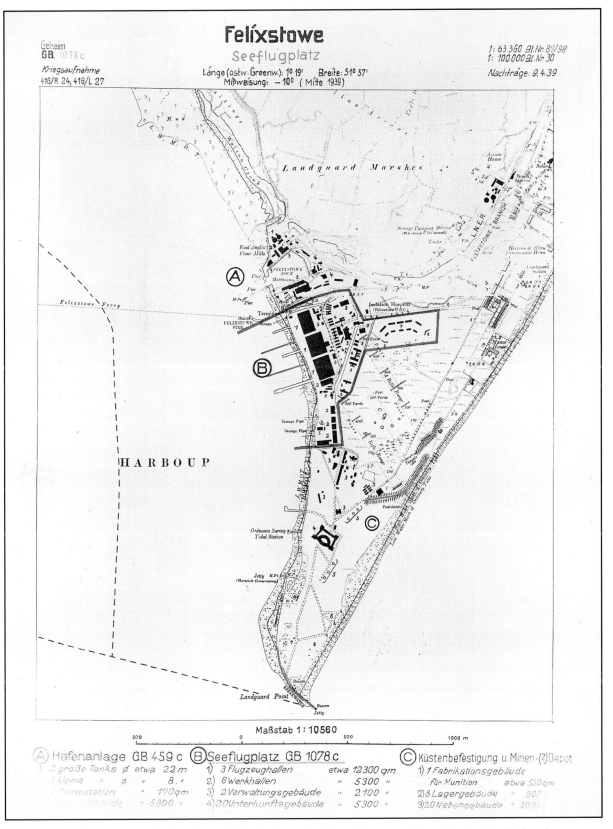

Felixstowe
Seeflugplatz

Geheim
GB. 1078 c

Kriegsaufnahme
416/R 24, 416/L 27

Länge (ostw. Greenw.): 1° 19' Breite: 51° 57'
Mißweisung: − 10° (Mitte 1939)

1: 63 360 Bl.Nr. 87/98
1: 100 000 Bl.Nr. 30

Nachträge: 9. 4. 39

Maßstab 1:10560

Ⓐ Hafenanlage GB 459 c   Ⓑ Seeflugplatz GB 1078 c   Ⓒ Küstenbefestigung u. Minen-(?)Depot

1) 2 große Tanks ø etwa 22 m	1) 3 Flugzeughallen etwa 12300 qm	1) 1 Fabrikationsgebäude
2 kleine " ø " 8 "	2) 6 Werkhallen " 5300 "	für Munition etwa 550 qm
2) 1 Pumpstation " 170 qm	3) 2 Verwaltungsgebäude " 2100 "	2) 8 Lagergebäude " 800 "
3) 1 Lagergebäude " 5300 "	4) 20 Unterkunftsgebäude " 5300 "	3) 20 Nebengebäude " 3000 "

118. A Luftwaffe target map showing the dock (A), the air station (B) and Landguard Fort (C), described below the map as 'Kustenbefestigung und Minen-Depot'. Dated 9 April 1939, it is based on the Ordnance Survey large-scale map.

119. The Pier Pavilion surrounded by barbed wire entanglements and other obstacles erected in 1940 to hinder the landing of troops on the beach. The pier was breached by Royal Engineers to prevent it being used by an invader, and a row of concrete blocks was placed across the beach to impede tanks that might be put ashore from landing barges.

120. The view from the pier during the Second World War, showing concrete anti-tank obstacles and barbed wire backed by scaffolding, all aimed at making life difficult for an invader. At extreme left can be seen the Suffolk Convalescent Home and Convalescent Hill.

121. A Second World War German map showing the boom at the entrance to Harwich harbour and various anti-aircraft gun positions (Flakstellung) and searchlights (Scheinwerfer) in the Landguard area.

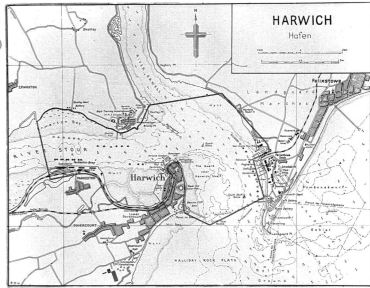

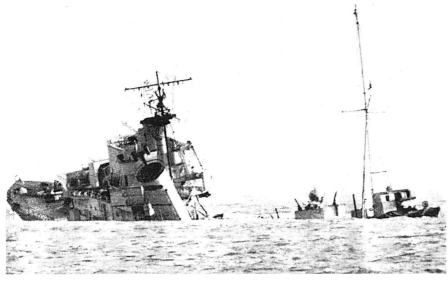

122. The shattered wreck of HMS *Gipsy* lying between the air station and Landguard Fort after she had been mined on 21 November 1939. She was leaving harbour with HMS *Boadicea* and the Polish destroyer *Burza* when a magnetic mine laid a few hours earlier by a German naval seaplane exploded under her keel, killing many of the crew and almost breaking the ship in two.

123. The menace of minelaying aircraft led to the construction of a number of offshore anti-aircraft forts which were floated out and sunk in shallow water on coastal sandbanks. The Roughs Tower was placed east of Felixstowe and was manned by a crew of seamen and Royal Marines; after the war it was abandoned, eventually to be taken over by a businessman who proclaimed the fort an independent principality under the name of Sealand. In the picture, taken in the 1980s, the remains of the fort's armament can still be seen.

124. Bawdsey Manor was sold to the Air Ministry in 1936 for use by Robert Watson-Watt and the scientists who had been developing radio-location, later known as radar, at Orfordness. It became the home of the first operational radar station, part of the Chain Home system that was to play such a vital part in the Battle of Britain. In the background of this photograph of dinghy sailing at Felixstowe Ferry in 1956 can be seen the four steel transmitter towers and three of the four wooden receiver towers of the Chain Home station. By this time the operations room and other vital parts of the station were accommodated in an underground bunker to the north of the manor, which continued to serve as the officers' mess until the station closed in 1990.

125. Besides carrying out trials of new aircraft, the air station staff had a hand in the development of marine craft used by the R.A.F., leading to the introduction of air-sea rescue launches employed to snatch aircrew from the water during the Second World War. This picture, taken at the Empire Air Day at the air station in 1938, shows a launch built by Brooke Marine at Lowestoft which clearly heralds the design of the wartime rescue launches.

Landguard Fort

At the south end of Felixstowe is a shingle spit known as Landguard or Langer Point which helps to protect Harwich harbour from north-easterly gales. As early as the reign of Henry VIII it was realised that an artillery emplacement on this point could serve to protect the harbour from attack by an enemy force.

The deep channel by which shipping enters the harbour lies close under the Suffolk shore, and guns placed on the point dominated the approach from the sea. The first defences were proposed in 1539 and two small bulwarks were constructed at 'Langar Point' and 'Langar Rood' in 1544; the second of these was probably at Walton Ferry, on the site occupied in the 19th century by Walton Battery.

It was only the prospect of war with Spain that persuaded the authorities to re-establish these 'decayed' fortifications, when in 1587 the Privy Council was warned that the Spaniards might seize the point, entrench themselves there and bombard Harwich. Not that these defences survived following the defeat of the Armada. Nothing more was done until 1626, when a simple square fort with an acute-angled bastion at each corner was built of turves laid like bricks.

With the outbreak of the Second Dutch War in 1665 the fort was repaired and orders given that it should be encased in brick, but these alterations were still incomplete when the Dutch attacked the fort on 2 July 1667. Just how many men landed on Felixstowe beach that day is open to question, but the force of soldiers and seamen probably numbered rather more than 1,600; it was a formidable raiding force, and had the little garrison of Landguard Fort not been reinforced by five companies of a regiment raised in West Suffolk, the Dutch might have achieved their aim of seizing the fort and forcing King Charles II and his Council to sue for peace.

As it was, a Dutch vessel which should have bombarded the fort from the sea went aground on the Ridge shoal, and the raiders were repulsed when they attempted to get their scaling ladders up against the walls of the fort. When a small English vessel sailed close to the fort and fired into the shingle, which flew up like shrapnel among the Dutchmen, the attack began to disintegrate.

Eventually the Dutch withdrew to their ships and sailed away. Had they obtained even a temporary foothold in Suffolk the future of the English monarchy would have been greatly in question. Thus, as Frank Hussey points out in his study of the attack, the visit made to Landguard Fort in 1668 by Charles II might have been something of a pilgrimage of personal thanksgiving. Captain Nathaniel Darell, who had been in command of the defending forces at the time of the attack, took the opportunity to present to the king a petition stating that 'his Company of his Royall Highness the Duke of York's Regiment in the said fort doe only fall sick for want of Bedds, Blanketts, & other accommodation wch he humbly prayed may be forthwith provided'.

The necessity for such a petition demonstrates the parsimony that both at that time and in later years hindered the development and maintenance of proper coastal defences, as much at Landguard as elsewhere. The mainly turf-walled fort was replaced in 1717-20 by a new one, described by Daniel Defoe as 'one of the best and securest in England', and this in turn gave way to an improved fortification 'in the form of a Pentagon with 5 Bastions and Curtains' in 1744-45.

The walls of the 18th-century fort can still be seen, incorporated in a casemated fortress constructed between 1871 and 1876. Mounting rifled muzzle-loading guns, the Victorian fort appeared impregnable. Its commanding officer in 1897, Major J. H. Leslie, wrote of it as 'a picture of ugliness, whilst its internal arrangements are by no means such as to conduce to the extreme comfort of its occupants'.

With batteries added outside the fort later in the 19th century, Landguard Fort continued to serve as part of the Harwich defences throughout two world wars. It ceased to have any part to play in Britain's defences when coast artillery was abolished in 1956, and the last soldiers marched out in 1957.

Today the Felixstowe Historical and Museum Society occupies the Ravelin block and arranges tours of the fort itself at summer weekends, but the long-term future of this historic monument remains uncertain. Plans to open it as a tourist attraction have not so far come to fruition.

One of the external batteries facing the sea is now a bird observatory, for Langer Common is a nature reserve which provides an important stopping place for migrants in spring and autumn.

126. The 16th-century bulwarks sited at 'Langer Point' and 'Langer Rood' were insubstantial constructions of earth and turf backed with wooden boards. The lack of permanence of such a sconce is evident from Peter Kent's reconstruction, and within 10 years both bulwarks had been reduced to ruin.

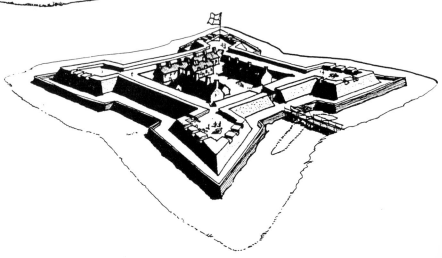

127. Landguard Fort as reconstructed in 1667 by Sir Bernard de Gomme, King Charles II's chief engineer. There had been time only to build a low brick scarp to form a fausse-braye, a secondary line of fortifications outside the main walls of the fort; when the Dutch landed on Felixstowe Common and attacked the fort on 2 July 1667. Though the fausse-braye was no more than ten feet above the bottom of the ditch, it proved an insurmountable obstacle to the attackers, who failed to get their scaling ladders up against the walls.

129. The interior of Landguard Fort in 1769, showing the gateway with a chapel over it. The house on the left with railings in front of it is the residence of the lieutenant-governor, vacated not many years earlier by Philip Thicknesse. To the right of the picture is Holland's Bastion.

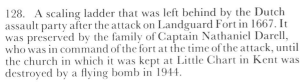

128. A scaling ladder that was left behind by the Dutch assault party after the attack on Landguard Fort in 1667. It was preserved by the family of Captain Nathaniel Darell, who was in command of the fort at the time of the attack, until the church in which it was kept at Little Chart in Kent was destroyed by a flying bomb in 1944.

130. Philip Thicknesse, who was appointed lieutenant-governor of Landguard Fort in 1753, and was dismissed, or resigned, in 1766. He is said to have introduced the tamarisk bush to Felixstowe, and it was he who turned a fisherman's cottage into a residence that was one of the earliest such establishments in Felixstowe. On his death in 1792 he left his right hand 'to be cut off after death, to my Son, Lord Audley, and I desire it may be sent him in hopes that such a sight may remind him of his duty to God, after having so long abandoned the duty he owed to a Father who once affectionately loved him'. What the estranged son thought of this bequest seems not to be recorded.

131. Landguard Fort shown on a print of 1753 after an oil painting by Thomas Gainsborough, who was befriended in his early days by Philip Thicknesse. It was across the rough common in the foreground that the Dutch forces advanced against the fort in 1667.

132. The casemates of Landguard Fort after the reconstruction of 1871-76, seen in a steel engraving published in 1888. At that time the fort was armed with four 12.5-inch rifled muzzle-loading guns and three 10-inch in the keep and two 10-inch in the three seaward casemates, an apparently mighty armament. The weakness of the fort was that there were insufficient guns covering the sea approaches. and in December 1888 work began on a new battery outside the fort.

133. An aerial view of Landguard Fort after the last soldiers had left in 1957. At the bottom of the picture are two six-inch gun emplacements, and towards top left is Darell's Battery surmounted by two director towers added in 1940. Beyond the walls of the fort is the Ravelin Block which now houses the Felixstowe museum.

The Air Station

During the First World War and right up to the outbreak of the Second World War, Felixstowe played a leading part in the development of marine flying, for much of the experimental work that resulted in the construction and operation of new types of marine aircraft was carried out at the air station situated between the dock and Landguard Fort.

The story of the air station began in 1913 when two naval aircraft created something of a sensation in the town by flying over the rooftops and then landing, one on the golf links and the other 'in a corner of Mr. Hobbs' mangold field the further side of Daffodil Wood, altering the appearance of a fine plant of root crops as it did so'. The year before, Commander Charles Samson had landed a seaplane in Harwich harbour and had based himself and his aircraft for some time at the naval training establishment at Shotley, though it was noted locally that he seemed to be taking a considerable interest in Felixstowe, and particularly in Landguard Common.

An announcement in April 1913 that a naval air station was to be established 'in Harwich harbour' did not specifically mention Felixstowe, but when Squadron Commander Charles Risk (who had been Commander Samson's observer the previous year) arrived on 5 August to commission the station, it was set up right next to Felixstowe Dock. The first aircraft, a Borel monoplane, arrived at Landguard on 2 October, closely followed by two other machines, one of which returned to its station at the Isle of Grain the same day.

Those early seaplanes were unreliable machines, and mishaps were not uncommon. The little Borel crashed in the harbour on 22 October 1913, and so was not available to give a demonstration to the First Lord of the Admiralty, Winston Churchill, later that same day; the crew of two were picked up safely by a tug and were able to describe the crash to Mr. Churchill over dinner in the Admiralty yacht *Enchantress* in the evening. Mr. Churchill himself suffered from the unreliability of such early aircraft when he made another visit to Felixstowe on 24 April 1914; the seaplane in which he was travelling was forced down by engine failure and he had to continue the journey in another aircraft sent from Felixstowe to pick him up from Clacton beach.

Such single-engined seaplanes were quite unsuitable for long patrols over the sea and had to confine their flying to coastal waters. They shared these patrols with the neighbouring Royal Naval Air Station at Great Yarmouth, 50 miles to the north. The ineffectiveness of the single-engined aircraft then in use was apparent to John Cyril Porte, who became the Commanding Officer at R.N.A.S. Felixstowe in 1915. He had already been concerned with the American aircraft designer Glenn Curtiss, who supplied two flying boats to the Royal Navy for patrol work in 1914. These two boats were sent to Felixstowe for trials, and while flying them on operations Porte discovered that they were suitable only for operation from smooth water; when conditions were in any way rough the flying boats would refuse to 'unstick'. Porte sought first to modify the existing hulls to improve their sea behaviour, and when that proved unavailing he arranged for a new hull to be built at Felixstowe incorporating the results of his own experiments. Porte's new hull was combined with the wings and tail of the Curtiss H.4 to produce the Felixstowe F.1, the first of a series of flying boats to carry the name of the base at which they were developed; those aircraft were destined to prove excellent workhorses for the Royal Naval Air Service, and later the Royal Air Force.

Porte and his chief technical officer, Lieutenant J. D. Rennie, not only redesigned the hulls of further American flying boats supplied to the R.N.A.S. but contributed a great deal to the development of successful marine aircraft. The Felixstowe flying boats carried out a system of patrols over the North Sea which was to be developed into the famous 'Spider's Web', a network that was to prove invaluable in the war against the U-boat; no fewer than 67 German submarines were sighted by flying boat crews from east coast stations in the last eight months of 1917, and 44 of them were attacked.

Flying boats were already a familiar sight at Felixstowe when in 1924 the station became home to the Marine Aircraft Experimental Establishment. Until the establishment moved to Helensburgh on the Firth of Clyde on the outbreak of war in 1939, the development of marine aircraft, both floatplanes and flying boats, was to be the role of the Felixstowe air station. Not only did every marine aircraft that entered service with the R.A.F. come to Felixstowe for evaluation but the station also played a vital role in the preparations for the series of Schneider Trophy races which culminated in Britain winning the trophy outright in 1931.

The air station was also concerned with the development of R.A.F. marine craft, the seaplane tenders and refuellers that provided an essential link with moored flying boats and the air-sea rescue launches that played such an important role during the Second World War by picking up ditched aircrew. One airman who was much involved in this work was a certain Aircraftman Shaw, who spent part of his R.A.F. service at Felixstowe; he was better known as Colonel T. E. Lawrence, or Lawrence of Arabia.

During the 1930s new types of aircraft that would play a vital part in the Second World War came to Felixstowe for trials and development. Among them was the prototype of the Short Sunderland, which was to help win the Battle of the Atlantic against German U-boats of a kind far more deadly than those that had operated in the North Sea in the First World War. Group Captain John Crosbie, who was then a test pilot at the M.A.E.E., recalls the interest that was aroused among holidaymakers on the pier when he piloted the Sunderland prototype in rough water trials off the Felixstowe seafront in 1938. He also took part in the trials of the less successful Saro Lerwick flying boat, which he found to be hydrodynamically unstable and which had a vicious swing on takeoff due to the torque of its two powerful Pegasus engines.

With the departure of the M.A.E.E. to the Clyde late in 1939 much of the air station was turned over to the Royal Navy, which based its Light Coastal Forces in the adjacent dock. The hangars were used for refitting the motor torpedo boats and other craft from HMS *Beehive*, as the naval base was known.

The men of HMS *Beehive* carried out both aggressive operations against heavily defended convoys making their way along the Dutch coast and defensive operations against German Schnellboote which carried out damaging attacks on the larger and more lightly protected convoys passing along the east coast. It was to counter the threat of these heavily armed miniature warships that the officers of HMS *Beehive* developed the motor gunboat and evolved new tactics which enhanced the fighting potential of these craft.

After the war the M.A.E.E. returned from the Clyde to its old home, but there was little activity at the air station apart from the testing of captured German aircraft. It was becoming apparent that the future lay with land-based aircraft, and the day of the flying boat was over. The air station was already nearing the end of its life when, in 1958, the Royal Air Force Station, Felixstowe, was granted the Freedom of Entry to the town by the urban district council. The Deed of Freedom was presented to the station commander, Wing Commander J. T. O'Sullivan, and was trooped through the ranks before the squadrons exercised their right of marching through the streets with bayonets fixed, colours flying, drums beating and bands playing.

The Royal Air Force ensign was lowered for the last time in 1962 and the quarters that had been used for so long by airmen were occupied for some time by the army. The Titan crane that had been installed in 1934 to handle flying boats was taken over by the Felixstowe Dock and Railway Company for loading heavy cargo into vessels which berthed on the end of the crane pier. Since then the entire air station has been taken over by the expanding dock, and the old apron on which so many aircraft had stood has been obliterated by the first container terminal.

134. Charles Samson taxies his Short S.41 towards the shed erected on the foreshore at Shotley during one of his visits in 1912. It was during these visits that he noted the suitability of Landguard Common for use as an air station.

135. Charles Samson in his normal flying kit poses for the photographer at the naval barracks at Shotley. He was one of the first four naval officers to qualify for their Aviators' Certificates, and was, in later years, to rise to a high rank in the Royal Air Force.

136. Four naval officers look on as seamen manhandle the Short S.41 on to the beach at Shotley. Charles Samson is standing on one of the floats, apparently tending a towline to a boat just visible on the extreme right.

137. Samson's Short S.41 after
alighting in the harbour.

138.   Charles Emeny's
photograph of a Maurice
Farman seaplane, probably No.
115, flying over Felixstowe pier.
On 19 May 1914, this seaplane
ascended to what was then
considered a record height of
8,300 ft.; 'the machine
appearing like a glittering
dragon-fly in the sky', according
to a local report.

139.   Maurice Farman No. 115 taxies towards the air station, its tail float churning the water.

140. The Borel monoplane No. 88 which crashed on 22 October 1913, while the first Lord of the Admiralty, Mr. Winston Churchill, was at Shotley naval barracks. According to the report in a local newspaper it sideslipped into the sea from a height of about 30 ft. 'due to the force of water as the machine skimmed over its surface having bent back the rocking lever arm into such a position that it was immovable'; this lever apparently worked the warping wires which twisted the wings to balance the aircraft, ailerons not being fitted at that time.

141. To enable the flying boats based at Felixstowe air station to take part in naval operations at considerable distances from home, special lighters were built to accommodate the machines. One of the lighters with a Felixstowe F.2A on board is shown here being towed at high speed by a destroyer of the Harwich Force. Later the lighters were fitted with a platform from which to fly off Sopwith Camel fighters as a protection against zeppelins during naval operations in the Heligoland Bight.

142. A Felixstowe F.2A flying boat taxiing in the harbour, seen from another flying boat, c.1917. Moored at bottom left is one of the special lighters built to carry flying boats on long-distance operations in the North Sea.

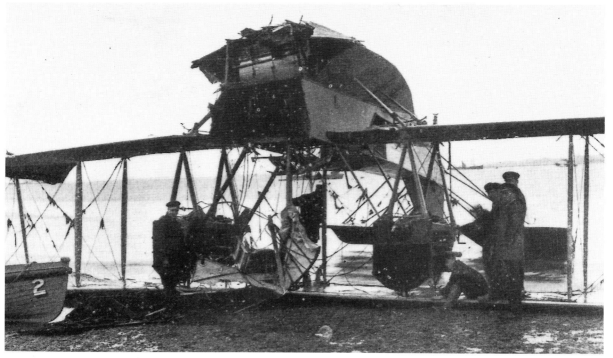

143. This Felixstowe flying boat was wrecked when it dived into the harbour when coming in to alight. The crew escaped with a ducking and were severely shaken. Crashes were by no means rare occurrences in the early years of flying, and not all crews were as fortunate as that of this flying boat.

144. A Sopwith Camel on its flying-off platform on a lighter being towed by a destroyer during operations. A Camel flown off in this way with Lieutenant S. D. Culley as pilot, shot down the Zeppelin L.53 one day in August 1918 during a naval operation in the Heligoland Bight. It was on this occasion that Rear Admiral Sir Reginald Tyrwhitt ordered the signal to be hoisted: 'See Hymns Ancient and Modern No. 224 verse seven'. This verse reads:

O happy band of pilgrims
Look upward to the skies
Where such a light affliction
Shall win so great a prize.

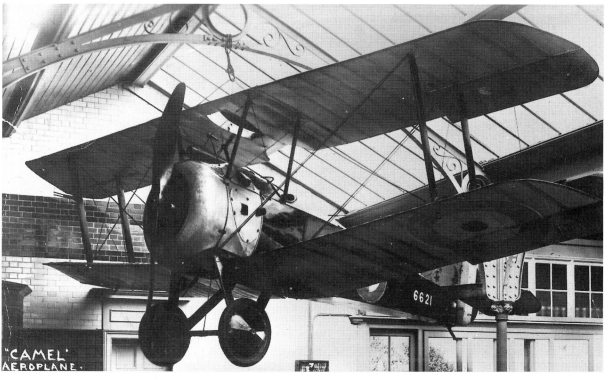

145. The Sopwith Camel in which Lieutenant Culley shot down the L.53 was displayed after the war in the Spa Pavilion at Felixstowe. It is now in the Imperial War Museum, London.

146. Manoeuvring one of the Felixstowe flying boats on the apron outside a hangar in 1918. The only way of getting a machine into the water was to manhandle it across the apron and down the slipway on a launching trolley; a crane was brought into use only in the 1930s.

147. Launching and retrieving machines in this way could be a very wet job indeed, and in later days special rubberised wading suits were issued to men engaged in such work.

148. Flying boats did not have the ability to attack high-flying zeppelins as their ceiling was too restricted, but in an attempt to counter the airships, an experiment was made with carrying a Bristol Scout on the upper mainplane of Porte Baby No. 9800. The pick-a-back aircraft separated successfully on 17 May 1916, the Porte Baby being captained on that occasion by Porte himself, but the combination was not used operationally.

149.   Another scheme for combating the zeppelins was to carry two Sopwith Schneider seaplanes aboard a submarine, the idea being that the seaplanes would surprise the airships before they had climbed to their operational height. In this photograph the submarine E.22 has submerged her stern so that one of the seaplanes can be floated on to the ramp built above the hull. Although the E.22 carried the aircraft on patrol the Schneiders never did go into action against an airship. It was found that the aircraft were unable to take off from the sea in rough weather.

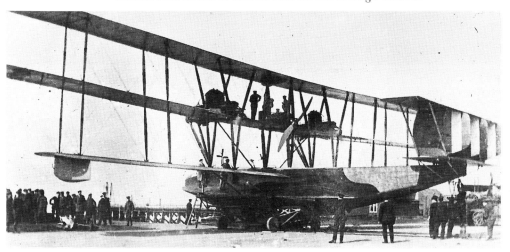

150.   Biggest of Porte's flying boats was the Felixstowe Fury, which had a wing span of 123 ft. and was almost certainly the first aircraft in the world to fly with power-operated controls in use. On one occasion this huge triplane took off from the harbour with no fewer than 24 passengers, fuel for several hours' flying and 5,000 lb. of ballast.

151.   Felixstowe pier and seafront seen in 1919 from the Felixstowe Fury. In the autumn of that year the Fury crashed on take-off with the loss of three members of her crew. One of the survivors of that crash was killed in 1920 when a Felixstowe F.5, which had earlier flown on a cruise to Scandinavia, went into a spin and struck the water off Felixstowe.

152. An aerial view of the air station during the latter part of the First World War, with jetties and slipways projecting out into the harbour. The three hangars erected in 1916-17 can be seen. The wave pattern on the left is made by a flying boat taxiing out.

153. The 50-ton Titan crane, installed at the air station in 1932-33 by Stothert and Pitt Ltd., seen lifting a Saro Severn flying boat. Four circular concrete columns were sunk in the bed of the harbour to support the structure, which became a well-known landmark. From the time of its installation until 1957 the crane was operated by Mr. Bill Duck, a former senior N.C.O. in the R.A.F.

154. A crane barge lifts the wreckage of the Blackburn Iris V from the water after it had sunk at its moorings one January night in 1933.

155. The fabric wing covering of the Blackburn Iris V hangs in tatters after the wreck had been brought alongside one of the air station jetties.

156. Part of the seafront, the gas-works, the dock and the air station can all be clearly seen in this view of three of the station's flying boats on their way to the 1934 Hendon Air Pageant. They are, from left to right, a Supermarine Scapa, probably the prototype S1648, Short Singapore and Saro London.

157.   The largest flying boat used by the R.A.F. in the biplane era, the Blackburn Perth, was tested at Felixstowe in 1934-36. The second of these aircraft to be built, K3581, is seen here on the apron with the centre engine and gravity fuel tank removed during investigation of a fuel flow problem. Group Captain John Crosbie, a pilot with No. 209 Squadron at that time, recalls that the Perth was 'a delightful machine to fly, apart from one nasty habit, a tendency to swing sharply to one side after touchdown'. He flew K5381 as co-pilot in 1935.

158.   One of the first production Short Sunderlands, L2160, flying over Walton Battery during trials at the M.A.E.E. which began in 1938. The prototype, K4774, was flown during testing at Felixstowe by Group Captain Crosbie, who was by then a test pilot at the M.A.E.E.

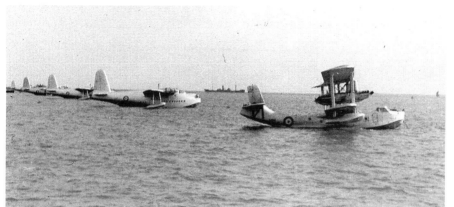

159. A Short Singapore III biplane flying boat and four Short Sunderlands lying on moorings off the air station, c.1939. The Singapore is probably K6922, which was sent to the M.A.E.E. in 1939 for squadron trials and was also employed in development work with the scientists at Bawdsey Manor who were perfecting the first radar warning system.

160. Two airmen in a motor dinghy watch the Short Mayo Composite aircraft *Maia* and *Mercury* taxi by during trials at Felixstowe in 1938. The smaller aircraft was designed as a mail-carrier for long-distance air routes, the intention being that with its heavy fuel load it should be lifted to operational height by the larger machine. Not only did this save the fuel that would be used in take-off and climb, but it enabled the *Mercury* to carry a load greater than its effective take-off weight.

161. The two aircraft arrived separately from the makers' works at Rochester, and the *Mercury* was then lifted on to its cradle above the hull of the larger machine by the Titan crane. Such work required extremely skilful handling by Bill Duck at the controls of the crane; he was adept at manoeuvring large flying boats within extremely close limits. Here the two machines can be seen together on the crane pier.

The Modern Port

At the end of the war the dock was so silted up that in places there was no more than six feet depth at low water, and trade had fallen away to next to nothing, though sailing barges still brought wheat from the London docks to the East Anglia Mills on the north quay. Facilities were few, and only the activities of two salvage companies salving material from ships sunk in 'E-Boat Alley' seemed likely to keep the Dock and Railway Company going for a while.

Then in 1951 the company was acquired by H. Gordon Parker, an agricultural merchant who was seeking a port through which he could export cargoes of barley to the continent without submitting to the difficulties of working within the National Dock Labour Scheme. For a mere £50,000 he acquired his own port, and the tiny labour force set about boosting the dock's income in any way possible.

The 1953 North Sea floods that drowned 40 men and women in their homes at Felixstowe, sweeping away caravans and tearing prefabricated houses from their foundations, did enormous damage to the dock facilities. While floodwater had ruined goods stored in the dock sheds, heavy seas had smashed gaps in the wooden entrance piers. Gordon Parker and his handful of employees set about getting the dock back into action, however, and it was not long before they were joined by a remarkable personality who was not only a fine leader but also an acute businessman: Ian Trelawney had already proved the quality of his leadership while serving with Coastal Forces at HMS *Beehive*. Buildings brought from wartime airfields in East Anglia and from a Ministry of Aircraft Production factory in North London were erected to provide storage space, and concrete from the runways of those same wartime airfields provided hardcore for roadways and tank bases. Ian Trelawney sought, and found, new trades to build up the port's business, and thanks to the good labour relations and the workforce's ready acceptance of new working methods, more and more shipping companies were attracted to the dock.

Ian Trelawney decided that the expanding plastics industry offered an opportunity and sought to cash in on the industry's need for solvents, a tank farm being developed for the handling and storage of these chemicals. Felixstowe not only pioneered the handling of industrial solvents but was at the forefront of other developments which revolutionised the shipping and ports industries, one of them being the introduction of containers.

In the 10-year period between 1964 and 1973 the total amount of cargo passing through the port rose from 376,669 tonnes to 3,463,425 tonnes, and by 1985 the total tonnage had reached more than ten million. In 1976 the Dock and Railway Company was acquired by European Ferries, which had been operating out of Felixstowe for some years in the guise of the Transport Ferry Service and Townshend Thoresen.

More recently the port has passed to Hutchison Whampoa, which also operates the great container port of Hong Kong.

162. In the 1950s the Felixstowe Dock and Railway Company was still recovering from the East Coast Floods of 31 January/1 February 1953, and trade was sought wherever it could be found. Here the motor barge *Edith May*, built as a spritsail barge by J. & H. Cann at Harwich in 1906, is loading ammunition in the dock on 27 May 1958. Skipper Bob Childs stands on deck.

163. There were no facilities such as quayside ladders at the dock in the early days and, in flagrant disregard of all safety regulations, dockers were lowered to vessels by crane, standing on a pallet. This photograph was taken in 1960 by Miss Paddy O'Driscoll, then mate of the motor barge *Edith May*. In the background can be seen East Anglia Mills on the north quay.

164.   A mobile crane is used to unload bags from a vessel in the dock in September 1964. Palletisation, one of the techniques pioneered at Felixstowe, had yet to come.

165. An aerial view of the tank farm which grew up to handle industrial solvents, methane and other imports. The original tanks were erected for the Admiralty in the early years of the century when the first oil-burning destroyers were introduced to the Navy. This side of the business had expanded so much by 1961 that a subsidiary company, Felixstowe Tank Developments Ltd., was established to take it over. The dock can be seen at upper left, and top right can be seen the Swedish Tor Line vesel which operated a passenger service to Gothenburg in the 1970s.

166. One of the Transport Ferry Service roll-on, roll-off ferries can be seen lying at No. 1 ro-ro berth in this aerial photograph taken in 1965, the year the berth came into operation. Between the berth and *The Little Ships*, formerly known as the *Pier Hotel*, is a marshalling area for the vehicles awaiting loading. The maltings behind *The Little Ships* was built in 1904-5 and was destroyed by fire in 1966.

167. Work began in 1966 on the construction of the first container terminal in front of the old air station hangars, which had been taken over by the Dock and Railway Company after the closure of the R.A.F. station four years earlier. The first container-handling crane, a Paceco Vickers Portainer crane, was in operation by July 1967. This first container terminal, later named the Landguard Terminal, has since been joined by others to the north of the dock, the Dooley and Walton Container terminals being added in 1981.

168. Felixstowe dockers turned the clock back on 7 April 1986, when the centenary of the dock was celebrated. Using a steam crane that had earlier been retired to a railway museum, they unloaded a cargo of timber from a sailing barge, while local dignitaries, also in period costume, looked on.

169. The Mayor and Mayoress of Felixstowe, Mr. and Mrs. John Mumford, arrived by coach in pouring rain for the centenary celebrations.

170. The millionth container to pass through the port is shown here being unloaded at the Walton Container Terminal in September 1988.

Bibliography

Corker, Charles, *In and Around Victorian Felixstowe* (A. Charles Phillips [Felixstowe] Ltd., 1972).

Hadwen, P., Twidale, R., and White, P., *Felixstowe: Views from the Past* (Published privately, 1985).

Hadwen, P., Twidale, R., and White, P., *Felixstowe: More Views from the Past* (Published privately, 1986).

Hadwen, P., Twidale, R., and White, P., *Felixstowe Memories* (Published privately, 1988).

Hadwen, P., Twidale, R., White, P., Henderson, G., and Smith, J., *The Hamlet of Felixstowe Ferry* (Published privately, 1990).

Hadwen, P., Smith, J., Twidale, R., White, P., and Wylie, N., *Felixstowe from Old Photographs: 100 years a Seaside Resort* (Published privately, 1991).

Hussey, Frank, *Suffolk Invasion: The Dutch Attack on Landguard Fort, 1667* (Terence Dalton, 1983).

Jobson, Alan, *The Felixstowe Story* (Robert Hale, 1968).

Kent, Peter, *Fortifications of East Anglia* (Terence Dalton, 1988).

Kinsey, Gordon, *Seaplanes Felixstowe* (Terence Dalton, 1978).

Leslie, Major J. H., *The History of Landguard Fort in Suffolk* (Eyre and Spottiswoode, 1898).

Malster, Robert, *Felixstowe: 100 Years a Working Port* (Felixstowe Dock and Railway Company, 1986).

Park, Cynthia, *The Cotman Walk* (The Felixstowe Society, 1982).

Symonds, E. H., *Trial by Air and Sea* (Published privately, n.d.).

Wood, *Landguard Fort* (Published privately, 1982).